Praise for
Champagne for the Soul

"The injunction 'Get real' usually means 'Leave your world of fantasy and return to what really is.' True realism always and everywhere is to find out where joy resides. In the past year this magical gift got lost or mislaid in my life. Mike Mason has located it, given it voice, and helped me recover it. Even one sip of *Champagne for the Soul* is a heady, exhilarating experience."

— BRENNAN MANNING, author of *A Glimpse of Jesus: The Stranger to Self-Hatred*

"Like the biblical writers, Mike Mason interprets 'joy' to be a central and basic expression of the Christian life. Convincingly, he takes us on a ninety-days' journey of joy, as he has experienced it within his own soul. Unlike the 'bubbly stuff,' it is lasting and transformative."

— JAMES M. HOUSTON, Founding Principal of Regent College and Board of Governors' Professor of Spiritual Theology

"Mike Mason has a felicitous gift for plucking perfectly ordinary words out of the mass of possibilities and distilling them into a kind of magic. Reading this book is like allowing champagne bubbles not only to rise, golden, in the flute, but to feel their tingling on your cheek and their intoxication flowing through your mouth and down your throat. This enchantment is Joy. Mason lives it and wants us to live it too—the joy of living and the joy of the Lord."

— LUCI SHAW, writer-in-residence at Regent College and author of *The Angles of Light*

"There is in Christ an open secret of constant joy. Natural depressive Mike Mason knows it well and here spells it out beautifully. Now tell me, who doesn't need that? So you, too, should soak your soul in this fine book."

— J. I. PACKER, professor, Regent College

"*Champagne for the Soul* shows me how to shake off my gloominess and enjoy the grace of God. This book is not only good advice, it's good theology."

    —TONY CAMPOLO, PH.D., Eastern University, St. David,
    Pennsylvania

"Whatever Mike writes, I read. Typical of this wonderfully titled book is this bit of wisdom: 'The greatest enemy of joy is fear.' Joy coexists with groaning, but it's real! Mike shows us the way from being caved in on ourselves to release in Christ."

    —LARRY CRABB, PH.D., author of *Shattered Dreams* and
    The Pressure's Off

CHAMPAGNE
for the
SOUL

OTHER BOOKS BY MIKE MASON

The Mystery of Marriage
The Furniture of Heaven
The Gospel According to Job
Practicing the Presence of People
The Mystery of Children

Celebrating God's Gift of Joy

CHAMPAGNE

for the

SOUL

MIKE MASON

WATERBROOK
PRESS

CHAMPAGNE FOR THE SOUL
PUBLISHED BY WATERBROOK PRESS
2375 Telstar Drive, Suite 160
Colorado Springs, Colorado 80920
A division of Random House, Inc.

Chapter 58, "Yabba-ka-doodles," appeared in a slightly different version in
Christianity Today, December 3, 2001, 42-44.

All Scripture quotations, unless otherwise indicated, are from the *Holy Bible, New
International Version*®. NIV®. Copyright © 1973, 1978, 1984 by International Bible
Society. Used by permission of Zondervan Publishing House. All rights reserved.
Scripture quotations marked (KJV) are taken from the *King James Version.* Italics in
Scripture quotations reflect the author's added emphasis.

ISBN 1-57856-692-4

Library of Congress Cataloging-in-Publication Data
Mason, Mike, 1952–
    Champagne for the soul : an experiment in joy / by Mike Mason.—1st ed.
      p. cm.
    ISBN 1-57856-692-4
    1. Joy—Religious aspects—Christianity.   I. Title.
    BV4647.J68 M37 2003
    241'.4—dc21
                          2002151436

Printed in the United States of America
2003—First Edition

10 9 8 7 6 5 4 3 2 1

for Joël and Daniel

In Memoriam

CONTENTS

I do not know what God wishes to do with me;
I am always very happy.

BROTHER LAWRENCE

———

When all your desires are distilled
You will cast just two votes:
To love more,
And be happy.

HAFIZ

———

AN EXPERIMENT IN JOY

I n October 1999 I began a ninety-day experiment in joy. I made up my mind that for the next ninety days I would be joyful in the Lord. Because this was an experiment, there was room for failure. If there were times when I wasn't joyful, I wouldn't despair or beat myself up. Rather I would gently, persistently return as best I could to my focus on joy.

So began (and continues to this day) the happiest time of my life. This book is the record of that experiment in joy, along with other thoughts on joy that came to me later. While I was astounded by the results of my initial experiment, I deliberately waited before writing a book. I knew my ideas needed time to mature, and more important, I had to see whether the new joy that had flooded my life would endure. Amazingly, it has. My original thesis turned out to be true: Joy is like a muscle, and the more you exercise it, the stronger it grows.

I've learned this the hard way because I haven't been a happy person by nature. Some people are, but I'm a bundle of nerves who has lived most of his life in a state of anxious, borderline depression. I didn't realize what was going on until my late twenties, when I finally crashed big-time and ended up in Alcoholics Anonymous. Later, when I'd been a Christian for ten years, I dropped into an even deeper depression.

So happiness has not been my strong suit, which is why I needed to experiment with joy. The way to break an addiction is to replace it with something stronger. To break my addiction to alcoholic spirits, I had to develop a taste for true spirituality. To break my addiction to the cheap wine of melancholy, I had to seek champagne for the soul.

Prior to this I'd tried other experiments in faith. I completed ninety days of peace, and I once committed to an entire week of not worrying. In the latter case I didn't have faith for ninety days, so I did the best I could. One nice thing about an experiment is that it's undertaken for a limited time. You don't have to be good forever, only for a day or seven days or ninety. Keep it up, and before you know it you're not trying to be good anymore, you're just good. Another virtue of an experiment is that it's just that—an experiment. It could fail. Though one makes a firm resolution to succeed if at all possible, the real point of an experiment is not to succeed but to inquire into the truth. Is it really possible to live every day in joy? I would never know if I didn't try.

Why ninety days? Because at least that long is necessary to effect a true change in character. What I wanted was not just a weather change but a climate change. A heroin addict once told me that after ninety days in Narcotics Anonymous, something happened to him: All at once, it seemed, his mind cleared of the dense fog of compulsions and untruths that had gripped him, and after that he was free. When I first began in AA, they told me to attend ninety meetings in ninety days. I went to more than a hundred. Anyone serious about breaking a grim addiction would do the same.

When the first seven days of my experiment in joy had passed and I was still joyful, I felt a miracle had taken place. Before this, a solid week of happiness—or even three days in a row—would have been unthinkable for me. Now, three years later, just as I've learned to be sober, I've learned to live in joy, and I believe the same is possible for any ordinary person.

I don't mean to imply that all ninety days of my experiment were smooth sailing. For about the first month I rode a wave of enthusiasm, but by the second month struggles had set in (as I knew they would), and I cannot say that I was happy all the time. Still, I discovered a new determination to face all challenges and to continue persistently probing for joy. During this time I learned that the search for joy is inseparable from spiritual warfare. Anyone who wants to be happy will have to fight for it.

In the final trimester of my experiment, while the struggles abated, a new enemy loomed—boredom. I grew so tired of always trying to be happy! Surely this is the bane of everyone who has ever sought to lay hold of joy. The way takes on a sameness, a tedium, a frightening narrowness. Yet I held on, and in the end I won through to a dimension of joy that I hadn't dreamed possible.

I hasten to add that I have not faced, either during my experiment or since, any dire personal tragedy. Does this fact invalidate my experiment? No, I don't believe so. Ordinary life is where most of us live most of the time, and it's just as difficult to be a joyful person in ordinary circumstances as in adversity. Petty problems can spoil joy as readily as big ones. Anyone who can find joy in a few ordinary things will surely find it everywhere.

Whether our problems are petty or big, this book asks the question: Is something missing from our Christianity? When the Book of the Law was lost in Old Testament times, it had to be reinstated by King Josiah. Today in the Western world we have no shortage of Bibles, but a key element of the biblical message—joy—has been lost. Listen to the prophet Joel: "The vine is dried up and the fig tree is withered; the pomegranate, the palm and the apple tree—all the trees of the field—are dried up. Surely the joy of mankind is withered away. . . . Has not the food been cut off before our very eyes—joy and gladness from the house of our God?" (1:12,16).

It's time for God's people to recover the joy of the Lord. Are you willing to try a ninety-day experiment? Will you join me in a bottle of champagne? There are many reasons in this dark and difficult world—many good reasons—not to be happy. This book will not dwell on those reasons. Rather, the bundle of paper you hold in your hands is a call to joy—a shameless, unmitigated challenge to throw off all worries and complaints and to "come and share your master's happiness" (Matthew 25:21). I want to convince you that today, this very moment, no matter who you are or what your circumstances, you can take hold of joy as simply as turning on a light switch in a dark room. With Paul I say, "Rejoice in the Lord always. I will say it again: Rejoice!" (Philippians 4:4).

Cheers!

BROKENNESS

Let me hear joy and gladness;

let the bones you have crushed rejoice.

PSALM 51:8

Do you have a favorite chair, a place you feel most at home and comfortable? So does joy. Joy's favorite chair is your sadness, your weakness, your grief. Wherever your wounds are most tender, joy finds a soft place to settle. A lighthearted person may rejoice, but no one has greater capacity for joy than one who is, like our Savior, "a man of sorrows, and familiar with suffering" (Isaiah 53:3). Joy loves our brokenness best.

One day in October, just before I began my experiment in joy, I received news that two teenage boys, the only children of friends of ours, had been killed in a car accident. This tragedy stunned me. These boys and their parents were exemplary Christians; no dangerous driving was involved, and no alcohol or drugs. The accident came with no warning, no apparent cause, no reason.

That night I lay awake, grieving and trying to process this disaster. Toward dawn, quite suddenly, the idea came to me to conduct a ninety-day experiment in joy. Coming out of the blue, this idea seemed not just irrelevant but wildly inappropriate. I was in no mood to rejoice. I thought of putting off the experiment until January, reasoning that a resolution to be joyful would make a good New Year's project. But the thing wouldn't be postponed; it had an energy of its own that carried me along, and the next day I began. I felt sure this was God's idea, not mine.

From the beginning, then, this project was all mixed up with suffering and loss. If you turn to the front of this book, you'll see that I've dedicated it to those two boys, Joël and Daniel. To dedicate a book is not just a matter of writing a name and some nice words. No, my book could not have been written without these boys. Like a muse, they accompanied me throughout my journey, and I feel their inspiration is somehow infused on every page.

Though at first this mingling of joy and tragedy made no sense, gradually I saw the wisdom of it. In the course of my experiment I came to understand three things.

First, Joël and Daniel are in heaven now, entirely happy with Jesus. Who better to inspire a book on joy than two saints who are drinking their fill of it right now and will forevermore?

Second, I saw that I deeply needed these boys, along with their grieving parents, to rescue me from the greatest danger of happiness, which is complacency. The one problem with happiness is its subtle tendency to distance one from worldly reality, especially from others who are unhappy. Sometimes during the writing of this book, when I happened to be with someone who was depressed or troubled, a cold shadow would pass through me upon realizing that I couldn't sympathize. I was too happy! And then I'd recall Joël and Daniel and their parents—and this holy family, half in heaven and half on earth, would restore human warmth to my heart.

Finally, I saw that if joy does not arise out of the midst of tragedy, it will not arise at all. Christian joy is rooted in darkness, chaos, meaninglessness, sorrow. Such joy isn't an airy ideal but a hard reality inextricably enmeshed with conditions in the real world. Separate joy from sorrow and there's nothing left. I had wanted happiness to be tidier than this, cleaner and more innocent. True happiness, however, is like our physical bodies, tidy on one side—the outer—and messy on the other. The happiest thought in the world is the shed blood of Christ.

REJOICE ALWAYS!

Rejoice in the Lord always.

I will say it again: Rejoice!

PHILIPPIANS 4:4

Throughout my experiment I made a point of telling people what I was doing. Often I heard the comment, "But surely a person can't be happy *all* the time?" While my ninety days were certainly characterized by ups and downs, I still wanted to answer, "Why not?" Why not accept the grand, stupendous gift of life like a big chunk of watermelon, letting the sweet, pink flesh melt in your mouth, and as for the rest, spit it out? Why gnaw away dolefully on seeds and rind?

Three years and many more ups and downs later, I continue to believe that nothing prevents a Christian from following the apostle Paul's charge to "rejoice in the Lord always." We're also exhorted to "always have hope" (Psalm 71:14), to "pray continually" (1 Thessalonians 5:17), to be "always giving thanks" (Ephesians 5:20), and to "keep all [God's] commands always" (Deuteronomy 5:29). Would Scripture set such high standards if they weren't possible? Jesus even said, "Be perfect, therefore, as your heavenly Father is perfect" (Matthew 5:48). The God of the Bible is a God of absolutes.

Consider the matter of love. Does anyone argue that we should love sometimes but not all the time? No, love "always protects, always trusts, always hopes, always perseveres" (1 Corinthians 13:7).

Or what about freedom? According to Jesus, "If the Son sets you free, you will be free indeed" (John 8:36). Do you want a little bit of freedom, or do you want to be free indeed? The kingdom of God is not for sometimes but for always.

In short, God wants us to be joyful indeed, rejoicing in Him always. The moment we hear this, we get stuck on that little word *always,* and our hearts sink. And so we overlook the key phrase "in the Lord." Nowhere does the Bible exhort us to do anything in our own strength, but only in the Lord. It would be cruel to expect anyone to be always happy apart from God. But "in the Lord"—why not? Who *wouldn't* be overjoyed with a God who "has given us everything we need for life and godliness" (2 Peter 1:3)? In the words of a Christmas carol, "Why should men on earth be so sad / Since our Redeemer made us glad?" If you have Christ, why not rejoice? If you don't have Christ, why not open your heart to Him?

Any happiness we think we've produced for ourselves will soon fade. The real thing comes from Beyond. Indeed it's the essence of joy to know that the Beyond is somehow contained within us. Knowing this, we know too that there will be no end to our joy, for we're connected to a Source that is limitless and eternal. Far from originating joy, humans are meant to be like an echo, reverberating with God's joy and sending it back to Him. The very word *rejoice* contains (in the prefix "re") this idea of "over again" or "back." The message of joy bears repeating, for in this dark world we need to hear about joy again and again. Paul obviously thought so when he wrote from a prison cell, "I will say it again: Rejoice!" True joy is tireless. It's like a little child squealing, "Do it again, Daddy!" to which our heavenly Daddy replies heartily, "Yes, let's do it again! And again and again!"

JUBILEE

Consecrate the fiftieth year and proclaim liberty throughout the land
to all its inhabitants. It shall be a jubilee for you.

LEVITICUS 25:10

A mong the rich family of words related to joy—including *joyful, joyous, enjoy, rejoice, jocund, jovial, jubilant*—is the word *jubilee*. In the Old Testament the Jubilee was a special yearlong celebration that occurred every fiftieth year. At least, this was the Lord's command. There's no record of the Israelites ever actually observing a Jubilee, and we in our commerce-driven society can easily understand why. In the Year of Jubilee all bondmen were to be freed, all agricultural land was to be left fallow, and all property was to revert free of charge to its original owners. The Jubilee was to be a Sabbath of Sabbaths, an entire year devoted to rest and freedom.

After centuries of refusing to observe this radical program, the Israelites were finally driven into exile for seventy years. The book of 2 Chronicles closes with a fascinating comment on this period: "The land enjoyed its sabbath rests; all the time of its desolation it rested, until the seventy years were completed" (36:21). Can you hear the sigh of relief in the land? Can you imagine the sigh in your own spirit if you took more time for rest?

The biblical Jubilee was like a yearlong experiment in joy. It was a fast from sadness and bondage, an invitation to set aside every other goal in order to enthrone pure joy as the centerpiece of life. What if we tried this in our culture? What if you tried it in your personal life?

God's idea of Jubilee was not that the other forty-nine years would be without joy, but that in order to live consistently in joy people must set aside times especially devoted to it. Because joy and freedom tend to get swept under the carpet by the dreary pragmatism of existence, periodically we need a shake-up. We need regular reminders of the central importance of joyous freedom in the Christian life.

If the Israelites had given the Jubilee its proper place, would they have returned afterward to business as usual? No, for an entire year of joy would have changed the tenor of their hearts. No doubt they'd have returned to buying and selling and working the land as usual, but this ordinary life would be so transformed that it would not seem ordinary anymore.

We need our Sabbaths and holidays. We also need more extended times of sabbatical. Rest is one of our basic requirements, and so is joy. We sleep regularly, but how regularly do we rejoice? Having grown so poor in the art of joy, shouldn't we be blocking out special times for its observance? Christmas is one such time, yet how often is the joy of Christmas crowded out by the season's busy demands?

Unobserved, joy languishes. All too easily we slip into believing that joy is unnecessary, that our days can readily flow along without it, or without much of it, and that perhaps life was never meant to be enjoyed but merely survived. Making joy a priority seems as radical as restoring all land to its original owners.

How do you think of joy? Is it like the Year of Jubilee—wildly impractical, even foolish, a quaint archaism described in a musty old book?

God's intention in the massive Jubilee land shuffle was clear: "The land must not be sold permanently, because *the land is mine*" (Leviticus 25:23). Your heart is also His. You're His child, and He intends you to be happy and free. Will you give Him back what is rightfully His and so take hold of the joy that is rightfully yours?

RIDING ON THE HEIGHTS

The LORD takes delight in his people;
he crowns the humble with salvation.
Let the saints rejoice in this honor
and sing for joy on their beds.

PSALM 149:4-5

I love this picture of the saints singing for joy on their beds. It reminds me that joy is restful, and that resting in the Lord is not a static but a dynamic activity. Jesus compared the kingdom of God to a farmer sowing seed: "Night and day, whether he sleeps or gets up, the seed sprouts and grows, though he does not know how. All by itself the soil produces grain" (Mark 4:27-28). Perhaps we avoid rest because we think of it as doing nothing, yet while we do "nothing," the Lord can accomplish His greatest work.

Before my experiment in joy, I thought I knew something of the value of rest. In order to sustain joy through ninety days, however, I had to allow more time for rest than ever before. No, that isn't quite accurate; it wasn't a matter of resting more, but of resting more frequently. Often I found that five or ten minutes of rest, snatched in the midst of activities I was impatient to pursue, were vital to renewing joy. Since before this I'd pictured myself as leading a contemplative lifestyle, it was a surprise to realize I was actually too busy, too driven, too reluctant to slow down and enjoy the refreshment of rest.

In the Bible joy and rest are intimately linked. "If you call the Sabbath a delight…then you will find your joy in the LORD, and I will cause you to ride on the heights of the land" (Isaiah 58:13-14). More than just a day of the week, the biblical Sabbath is an attitude of heart. I find the soul of rest beautifully expressed in these words by novelist Robert Cormier: "Don't frown, don't be worried, don't be unhappy. God is letting you discover Him. Meanwhile let the days bring you what they will and don't fuss or fret about who you are or what you are. Let the days come, the darkness and the light, and don't concern yourself."[1]

When Bertrand Piccard and Brian Jones became the first men to circumnavigate the globe in a balloon, they said the secret of their success was not to conquer but to harmonize with the winds. All they had to do was "let Mother Nature take us in her arms, carry us around the world, and set us gently back down again."[2]

This is really all there is to the life of joy. Throughout my experiment I noticed that whenever I felt worried or pressured about whether I was happy enough, joy eluded me. It is not the way of joy to be grasped. Rest is like unclenching a fist, letting go of the need to do or to know, in order that receiving might take the place of grasping. If we aren't willing to rest, God will arrange rests for us, because He doesn't want us to rush through life but to enjoy it.

One interesting property of happiness is that we cannot be happy without knowing it. We can be many other things—rich, blessed, lucky, loved—and not know it, but to be happy we must know it. The awareness is a part of the happiness. Rest is an opportunity to become aware of joy. We need sleep because we need dreams, and we need rest because we need daydreams. Many people's lives are so unhappy that their only glimmers of joy come in daydreams.

In Deuteronomy we read that the Promised Land "is not like the land of Egypt...where you planted your seed and irrigated it by foot," but is "a land of mountains and valleys that drinks rain from heaven" (11:10-11). Is your soul drinking rain from heaven, or are you laboriously hauling brackish water from a distant, exhausted well?

GOING FOR THE GOLD

The kingdom of heaven is like treasure hidden in a field.
When a man found it, he hid it again, and then in his joy
went and sold all he had and bought that field.

MATTHEW 13:44

What treasure is so great that a man would give everything he has to obtain it? Jesus calls it "the kingdom of heaven," and the key to it is the gospel.

What is the gospel?

I was once asked this question by a tormented young man who had been a Christian for many years and had just completed a three-year course of study at one of the best evangelical seminaries in the world. At the time, the Lord did not give me an answer for him. What could I say to someone who was already so stuffed with theology? Yet all his knowledge couldn't keep him from being racked by guilt—guilt about all his weaknesses, about all the unfortunate people in the world, about the feebleness of his love, and so on.

Of course, underneath all this guilt was anger. A more troubled fellow I've seldom met. At the same time, he struck me as somewhat typical of the North American Christian, only more honest than most in his perplexity. How many of us really know the gospel, or live as if we do?

In the parable of the treasure hidden in a field, Jesus' purpose was not to explain the gospel in theological terms but rather to emphasize its dramatic effect on the believer. "In his joy," we read, the man in the story gave up everything he had in exchange for his newfound treasure. He would never have done this for the sake of doubt or guilt, which are poor motivators. Though a man may feel ever so justified for his doubts, and though he may feel ever so virtuous about the load of guilt he carries—for doesn't this show how well he understands his sinfulness?—still such feelings can never motivate him to live as God wants him to.

To follow and obey God, we need joy. We need to catch a glimpse of the greatest treasure of all—the "inexpressible and glorious joy" (1 Peter 1:8) of believing in Christ.

It may seem a tall order to live every day in joy. Yet think of the prize to be won—a world washed new, a heart clean and pure, a spring in the step, boundless hope, an irresistible impulse to laugh and sing. What would you give to attain such treasures? More to the point: What wouldn't you give?

The man in the parable gave up everything for joy. He gave all to gain all. What keeps us from doing the same? No doubt we can think of many hindrances, but really there's only one—lack of faith in the gospel's joy. We listen to our heart, we sense the stirrings of the Holy Spirit, and we begin to sense a joy so delicious and otherworldly that immediately we presume there must be some catch. We think joy is like sugar or chocolate and we're only allowed so much. Surely such a wonderful feeling isn't meant to be ours? Surely we aren't permitted to live this way? And so, unlike the man in Jesus' parable, we stop short of going for the gold.

How do I know that I know the gospel? I know it by the joy it gives me. By contrast, I know I've lost sight of the gospel when I find myself restless, unhappy, fearful, plagued by subtle guilt. Unhappiness keeps me stuck. Only joy moves me over the line into experiencing the kingdom of heaven.

Now answer for yourself: What is the gospel? Keep asking until the answer that comes provokes an eruption of joy.

WHAT HAPPENED?

What has happened to all your joy?

GALATIANS 4:15

Notice the clear implication in Paul's dramatic question above: Christians should be living a life of joy, and if we aren't, something's wrong. If we aren't joyful we need to ask ourselves, *What happened?* Where did we get off track? Paul's letter to the Galatians is all about how these early Christians moved away from the gospel of joy and freedom, and what they needed to do to come back.

Another implication of Paul's question is that the Christian life always begins in joy. If we've lost sight of joy, regaining it is a simple matter of retracing our steps, going back to where we first opened our hearts to Jesus. The good news of Christ is so wonderful that it's always received with joy. As Paul wrote elsewhere, "You welcomed the message with the joy given by the Holy Spirit" (1 Thessalonians 1:6). This is why people come to Christ—because they sense the great joy He alone offers. Just before sinners repent they can sense the peace, the freedom, the immense relief of handing over everything to Jesus. And so they let go and let God, and He is true to His word and floods them with joy.

No one would become a Christian if this hard decision were not accompanied by stupendous joy. Granted, depending on temperament and circumstance, for some the joy of conversion may seem more intellectual, while for others it's more emotional. Some see their conversion as a gradual process, while others recall a dramatic experience. Each one receives joy in his or her own way. Still, every true conversion to Christ is marked by joy.

Moreover the joy of conversion is no flash in the pan. It keeps coming and coming. Many Christians can look back on the early days of their faith as a season in which the whole world seemed new. Colors were brighter, music was richer, relationships deepened, some struggles were overcome almost with ease. Why *shouldn't* this be the case for someone who has been born again into eternal life? "I am making everything new" (Revelation 21:5) is a promise of Jesus that every Christian experiences from the start. We indeed enter "a new life" (Romans 6:4).

Paul's question, therefore, is a valid one: What happened to all this? What would possess anyone to throw it away? Don't you remember the glorious joy with which you first welcomed the Lord Jesus Christ? Why would you settle for anything less now? Are you less of a Christian today than you were at conversion? No, if anything you should be further along; you should feel more joyful, more free, more blessed in every way. What rigid rules and petty pieties are cutting you off from joy? As Paul wrote exasperatedly, "You foolish Galatians! Who has bewitched you?... You were running a good race. Who cut in on you and kept you from obeying the truth?" (3:1; 5:7).

The very fact that we want joy proves that we know what it is. We know it because we had it once, and if we had it once, we can have it again. How did it arrive in the first place? By faith. By hearing and believing the astounding message that "the only thing that counts is faith expressing itself through love" (Galatians 5:6).

FIRE FROM HEAVEN

Fire came out from the presence of the LORD and consumed
the burnt offering and the fat portions on the altar.
And when all the people saw it,
they shouted for joy and fell facedown.

LEVITICUS 9:24

This verse is the first significant mention of joy in the Bible. The book of Leviticus can seem dull reading, but the result of all those dreary rituals and sacrifices was that the people "shouted for joy and fell facedown." Why? Because suddenly they received the goal of all their faith—to be with God. Fire came down from heaven and consumed their sacrifice, burning away everything that separated them from God, assuring them that their sins were forgiven and that they were holy.

Joy is a response to the Lord's presence. The people rejoiced because God responded to them, kindled their sacrifice. Has the fire of God come down and consumed your sacrifices? All your piety, your churchgoing, your repentance, your efforts to be good—do these produce shouts of joy? If not, something's wrong; your sacrifice isn't complete.

Repentance consists of two parts, but many people settle for only the first part. Repentance means to turn, but many get stuck halfway. The first part of repentance is to turn away with loathing from sin; the second part is to turn toward all the good things God offers in exchange. Indeed it's impossible to turn away from greed without turning toward generosity, to put aside lust without taking up love, or to escape bitterness without embracing celebration.

It's easier to let God's law convict than to let His gospel set free. Two great obstacles to joy are guilt and grudge: Either we feel guilty about our own sin, or we bear a grudge against someone else. In each case we fail to grasp the gospel, which teaches that both conditions are entirely unnecessary, for they can be readily healed through forgiveness—either receiving it for ourselves or extending it to another. The prerequisite for forgiveness is our repentance.

What was the purpose of the sacrificial system in the Old Testament? Did the slaughtering of animals bring satisfaction to God? No, for as David prayed, "You do not take pleasure in burnt offerings" (Psalm 51:16). What then did God expect from all those messy sacrifices?

He wanted His people to be happy. He wanted them to go away from these rituals feeling joyful and free, knowing that their sins had been dealt with and would not return to haunt them. Unconfessed sin blocks joy; therefore the complex details of the sacrificial system were designed to enable people to acknowledge and express sorrow for specific sins. The real goal, however, was not to make the people sorry but to make them happy. God wanted them to know the ultimate happiness of being so thoroughly cleansed from sin that they could waltz right into His throne room and be with Him forever. The blood of animals could not accomplish this goal perfectly, but the blood of Jesus has. Now without any rituals "we have confidence to enter the Most Holy Place by the blood of Jesus" (Hebrews 10:19). This is better than fire from heaven.

Repentance is the key that turns all darkness into light. After all, it's how our Christian life began, how the joy of the Lord first came to us—through confessing our sin and turning to Christ. How do you feel today about being a sinner? Does knowing the truth about yourself shame or anger you, or does it bring you a profound and happy relief? Many people grow tired of repenting because it doesn't seem to make them happy. Yet full repentance is a joyful act in itself. If we're not joyful, we haven't finished repenting. The sign that we've repented well is happiness, as God consumes our sacrifice of sorrow and exchanges it for joy.

MIRTH

The disciples were overjoyed when they saw the Lord.

JOHN 20:20

How did the disciples express their great joy upon being reunited with the risen Jesus? Did they clap hands and dance? Collapse in hysterical laughter on the floor? Punch fists in the air and yell "Yippee!"? What do people do when they are, as the above verse puts it, "overjoyed"?

We find a hint in Acts 3:8, when a lame beggar, healed by the power of Jesus, enters the temple "jumping, and praising God." There's another hint in Acts 12:14, when a Christian servant girl named Rhoda hears a knock at the door and is amazed to be greeted by the apostle Peter, who's supposed to be in prison: "When she recognized Peter's voice, she was so overjoyed she ran back without opening it and exclaimed, 'Peter is at the door!'" Imagine being so happy about a visitor that you forget even to open the door. Excess of joy can cause people to lose their wits, act strangely, do silly things.

One of the happiest saints who ever lived, Brother Lawrence, confessed that the joy of the Lord at times so overpowered him that he would "cry out, singing and dancing violently like a madman." An observer reported that "for almost thirty years his soul was filled with interior joys so continual and sometimes so great that to contain them and prevent their outward manifestation, he had to resort to behavior that seemed more foolishness than piety."[3]

When I asked a joyful friend to define joy, without batting an eye he responded, "Joy is a deep-seated sense of well-being, often arising in mirth." Both parts of this definition are significant. Without a deep sense of well-being, one cannot achieve the release from self-consciousness that is joy's prerequisite. Similarly, it's doubtful if true joy can exist without regular expressions of spontaneous mirth. Joy by nature overflows and becomes "overjoyed." Irrepressible, it needs an outlet, needs to burst forth in laughter, dance, song, bizarre behavior, jollity.

During my experiment I was sometimes so happy that I'd stride down the street gleefully chanting, "Oh God, You're too good to me! Life's never been so good!" Other times I'd laugh till I ached, dance around the house to music, or lie flat on my back unable to move because the bliss was so great. Each time I'd think that I couldn't possibly hold any more joy—and then my joy would increase! God cannot be outdone. It's the nature of His joy to keep expanding. It's bigger than we are, and we can't possibly hold it all.

Of all the books of the Bible, Psalms, though filled with anguish, expresses the most mirth. Here the very "hills are clothed with gladness" and the valleys "shout for joy and sing" (65:12-13). Psalm 65 was penned by David, that great king so abandoned to joy that he danced half-naked in the streets before the Ark of the Lord. How do we picture his dancing? Solemnly worshipful, stately, majestic? More likely it was an overflow of mirth, full of fun-loving capers, calflike gambols, pure *joie de vivre*.

Some of the most mirthful people, I've noticed, have suffered tragic losses. When the stories start flowing about some dear departed loved one lost to cancer, the macabre jokes and the grisly merriment can be shocking to an outsider. However, overwhelming emotions must have some release, and healthy mourning may include crazy laughter. If we're meant to "rejoice in the Lord always," then mirth is always in season.

THIS IS THE DAY

This is the day the LORD has made;

let us rejoice and be glad in it.

PSALM 118:24

Three old men, Al, Ed, and Joe, sat on a park bench.

"Isn't it amazing," said Al, "that at my age I still feel wonderful!"

"That so?" responded Ed. "And to what do you attribute your well-being?"

"I think," reflected Al, "it's probably because I have sex twice a week."

"How interesting!" said Ed. "I too am enjoying wonderful health."

"And what's your secret?" asked Al.

"My secret, I'm sure, is that I have sex three times a week."

At this point Al and Ed noticed that Joe was smiling broadly.

"What are you so happy about?" the other two asked.

With a sigh of deep joy Joe responded:

"I have sex once a year. And today's my day."

When I first heard this joke I laughed and laughed, and it kept me chuckling for days. Usually at the heart of a good joke lies a grain of truth. The truth in this joke is that Joe, even though he has sex only once a year, is still far better off than the other two fellows. Why?

Because today's his day!

Joe is the sort of fellow who lives for the pleasure of each day. Today his pleasure is in lovemaking. Tomorrow it will be in something else, and the next day something else again. Joe has no method or system for what will bring happiness. He knows that well-being doesn't lie in something that happens three times a week, or four times, or every day. No, Joe's only secret is that he's free—free to enjoy each day for what it is. That's why he's sitting there smiling so contentedly. The other guys have their off days, but Joe is in love with today. He knows that joy inhabits the present moment.

One of my favorite sayings comes from Saint Herman of Alaska: "From this day, from this hour, from this minute, let us love God above all." Every moment we can cross over a line into the country of joy. You may not have been happy when you picked up this book today, and you cannot predict that you'll be happy tomorrow or next week. But right now, lifting your eyes to this glorious day God has created, you can rejoice in it.

The present, after all, is the only time over which we have any control. I can't control the past; it's gone. As for the future, I don't know what will happen. Right now, however, I can choose to rejoice and so transform my life. A decision to rejoice in the present changes not only the present, it also changes my view of the past and ignites my future with hope. Thus there is power in the present moment, and only in the present, to transform all of time.

Perhaps it's too much to expect anyone to live an entire life of joy. Yet is it too much to be happy for one moment? The only way to eat an elephant is one bite at a time. The mountainous project of life must be broken down into manageable steps. That's why God, before He created anything else, created days: "And there was evening, and there was morning—the first day" (Genesis 1:5). Even the monumental work of creation was handled according to the homespun precept, "One day at a time."

Don't put off happiness until tomorrow—it might not wait for you. The time to enjoy life is now.

TEN JOYFUL
COMMANDMENTS

Shout for joy to the LORD, all the earth.
Worship the LORD with gladness;
come before him with joyful songs.

PSALM 100:1-2

We're all familiar with the Ten Commandments of Exodus, but do you know the ten commandments of Psalm 100? This psalm is entirely written in the form of commands. The first three are listed above. The other seven are: "Know that the Lord is God"; "[Know that] it is he who made us"; "[Know that] we are his people, the sheep of his pasture"; "Enter his gates with thanksgiving"; "[Enter] his courts with praise"; "Give thanks to him"; "Praise his name."

But wait a minute. Didn't we leave behind all those Old Testament commandments when we "died to the law through the body of Christ" (Romans 7:4)? As Christians, don't we come to God by faith rather than works? Actually, the New Covenant is as full of laws and commands as the Old. Indeed the new commands are even more exacting than the old, for they include interior rules such as "Do not let your hearts be troubled" (John 14:1), "Be completely humble and gentle" (Ephesians 4:2), "Be clear minded and self-controlled so that you can pray" (1 Peter 4:7), and "Rejoice in the Lord always" (Philippians 4:4). To this list might be added the ten commandments of Psalm 100.

Each phrase of this psalm is either a direct command to rejoice or a command to do something that results in joy. For example, if we know for certain that we belong to God, that "we are his people, the sheep of his pasture," how can we not "worship the LORD with gladness"? Happy people, secure in knowing they belong, are free to worship their Creator with abandon. Unhappy people withhold worship, which is the very reason for their unhappiness.

Joy is a biblical commandment. Is it fair for God to command you to be happy? Aren't the odds overwhelmingly stacked against you? No, this is a lie. The truth is that Jesus has done everything to secure your happiness, in order that His "joy may be in you and that your joy may be complete" (John 15:11).

Nobody questions Jesus' most important command, "Love one another" (John 13:34). Why then do we argue with the command to rejoice? In the case of love, we know that we ought to do it, and we also know that we can. If we don't love, it's not because we cannot but because we will not. Simple as that.

It's the same with joy. Happiness is a choice. As Abraham Lincoln put it, "People are just about as happy as they make up their mind to be." What we lack as Christians isn't just the will to believe the gospel, but the will to be happy about what we believe. Indeed our lack of joy is a sign of unbelief.

Part of my purpose in writing this book is to demonstrate that happiness is not happenstance, but rather it involves a profound spiritual discipline. If I want to be strong, I don't sit around waiting until I'm strong enough to lift weights; rather, I lift weights in order to become strong. To accept joy as a commandment is to admit that it doesn't come to one effortlessly but requires the cooperation of the will to achieve. Like salvation, joy is a free gift of God that cannot be earned, yet even a gift must be opened and actively enjoyed by the recipient. It takes energy to "shout for joy to the LORD," but it takes just as much energy (or more) to be miserable. Why not rechannel our efforts into something more fun?

REDEFINING HAPPINESS

So the women hurried away from the tomb,
afraid yet filled with joy.

MATTHEW 28:8

I s joy a feeling? Yes, but it has many nuances, and it can also be mixed with other feelings. From the verse above we see that joy can be mixed with fear and still be joy. From many other verses we know that joy mixes well with suffering. Sometimes joy feels like letting go when we're overwhelmed. Sometimes it feels more like an underlying confidence or courage. Sometimes joy is what seeps through the cracks when our hearts are breaking.

This isn't to say that joy can be mushed together into any old feeling at all. No, joy is distinct, so distinct that it can be separated from other feelings, though often we're reluctant to do this if the other feelings are strong. When joy is colored sad, it's because in the midst of sadness it comprehends something greater. When joy is mixed with fear, it's because it smells victory in the offing. When joy's heart breaks, it's because joy feels free and safe enough to embrace everything, even the feeling of falling to pieces.

I don't want to lie in this book. I don't wish to give the impression that throughout my experiment in joy I was exuberantly happy every minute of every day, nor that this was even my goal. No, I continued to have moods—frustration, boredom, melancholy, anxiety, anger. Nevertheless joy kept returning like the ocean's tide to wash my soul. Even *returning* isn't the right word, for in a happy soul joy never really goes away, but remains like something just out of focus in the background of a photograph, or like a sepia wash that changes the tone of the whole picture.

Perhaps we need to rethink our definition of happiness. If we're going through a difficult time and our definition of happiness says we must always feel wonderful, then we have a no-win situation. We may need to modify our definition to something along the following lines:

Happiness is doing my best in bad circumstances.

Happiness is knowing I can overcome anything.

Happiness is cutting myself lots of slack.

Happiness is appropriating God's grace and mercy in such a way that I don't feel pressured to perform.

And so on. During my experiment I had to look closely at what joy actually feels like in practice. God kept changing my view of it, showing me more and more angles, with the result that joy became more readily accessible to me in all manner of situations. If I'm looking for a perfectly clear crystal stone on a beach, I may not find one, but if I look for the crystalline in stones, I'll see it gleaming everywhere.

It takes wiliness to be happy. When cornered, we have to look at all the options and find the way out. We have to know how to outwit the heebie-jeebies, how to think faster than our blackest thought. We must be able to slip the nooses of condemnation, lethargy, self-pity, confusion.

Joy may seem an upbeat sort of feeling, but the direction of joy isn't always up. Often to be joyful we must go down—down through the noise of racing thoughts, down through the swirling chaos of circumstances, down through the deceptive appearances of life, down into the still waters and green pastures at the heart's core.

Have I been happy today? Yes, richly so. Yet I've also been processing deep undercurrents of disturbing feelings. Can these two states coexist—joy and profound disturbance? Strange to say, they can. An unsettled joy isn't the same as a clear, singing joy, but it's joy nonetheless. Though there be clouds in the sky, the sun can still shine brilliantly.

BE HERE NOW

I commend the enjoyment of life, because nothing is better
for a man under the sun than to eat and drink and be glad.
Then joy will accompany him in his work all the days
of the life God has given him under the sun.

ECCLESIASTES 8:15

For such a notoriously gloomy book, Ecclesiastes has a great deal to say about happiness. Indeed a careful study of this book shows that happiness is its central theme. In various ways the author keeps saying, "There is nothing better for men than to be happy" (3:12).

If we find Ecclesiastes gloomy, it's because the writer rubs our noses in the great enemy of happiness, ennui. Call it angst, world-weariness, or a sense of futility, this is the condition that overtakes the person who has everything except happiness, the been-everywhere-done-everything sort who is tired of living.

This is the story of Ecclesiastes. After trying it all—money, women, drink, power, ambitious projects, all the worldly pleasures including even the gathering of wisdom—the author admits, "I hated life" (2:17), and he sums up everything with his favorite word: "Meaningless! Meaningless!" (1:2).

In Ecclesiastes, life is meaningless not in the sense of being devoid of meaning, but in the sense that its meaning cannot be fully deciphered: "No one can comprehend what goes on under the sun. Despite all his efforts to search it out, man cannot discover its meaning. Even if a wise man claims he knows, he cannot really comprehend it" (8:17). In this book even happiness itself is meaningless. Open your eyes and look around at this world of pain, and then try to justify being happy. It can't be done. Joy is not rational; its mystery cannot be plumbed; no philosophy leads there. Some circumstances may hold reasonable grounds for joy, but to rejoice always—this is beyond reason, beyond understanding.

What to say, then, to the person overcome by meaninglessness and the tedium of life? Is it still possible to rekindle joy? The writer of Ecclesiastes says yes, but he doesn't say how. Rather than explaining how to be happy, he simply cries out: Be happy! Stop trying to figure it all out, and just enjoy what's under your nose. "Better what the eye sees than the roving of the appetite" (6:9). It's not what you look at that matters, but how you see. You've tried everything else—now try enjoying your life exactly as it is.

Of course the profound simplicity of this message is lost on our sophisticated minds. We cannot grasp it until we enter into the mystery of meaninglessness. Ecclesiastes cuts the ground from under all those who would meaningfully plan or scheme for happiness, as if it were something we could obtain if only we were good enough or smart enough or careful enough. The book of James scorns those who say, " 'Today or tomorrow we will go to this or that city, spend a year there, carry on business and make money.' Why, you do not even know what will happen tomorrow" (4:13-14). Don't we approach happiness this way? We tell ourselves, "Tomorrow I'll do such-and-such and it will make me happy," or, "After I finish work today, then I can relax and be happy."

Nonsense. Be happy now! If you can't find happiness in the present moment, you never will. Joy isn't around some corner—it's here.

THE SECRET OF
HAPPINESS

When God gives any man wealth and possessions,
and enables him to enjoy them, to accept his lot
and be happy in his work—this is a gift of God.
He seldom reflects on the days of his life, because
God keeps him occupied with gladness of heart.

ECCLESIASTES 5:19-20

The passage above applies personally to me. While I'm not rich by some standards, I know that globally I'm among the top 3 percent of the world's wealthy. And so, most likely, are you. For my part, I also happen to love my work. With two such amazing blessings, why shouldn't I be happy?

By God's gift, I am. However, my happiness has also been hard won, for simply being well-off and loving one's work do not ensure happiness. Indeed I was financially comfortable and loved my work for many years before I became happy about it. According to Ecclesiastes, the key factor in happiness is not the possession of good things but rather the ability to enjoy what one has by accepting one's lot.

Whether rich or poor, one may just as easily be trapped by covetousness, the sin of despising one's lot. To covet is to crave what one does not, often cannot, have. By contrast Paul states, "I know what it is to be in need, and I know what it is to have plenty. I have learned the secret of being content in any and every situation" (Philippians 4:12). The poor may think that if only they had more money they could be happy, but the rich think this too. As

Ecclesiastes succinctly puts it, "Whoever loves money never has money enough" (5:10).

Similarly in the case of work, even the grandest job in the world can grow stale, as King Solomon discovered for himself. How ironic that the most fortunate man on earth had to learn to be happy by embracing his own circumstances. Most of us tend to look for happiness in the results of our work, but according to Ecclesiastes it's not to be found there: "What does man gain from all his labor at which he toils under the sun?" (1:3). Rather, pleasure must be found in the work itself: "I saw that there is nothing better for a man than to enjoy his work, because that is his lot" (3:22).

If it's not money or a job that people covet, it's power or fame or romance or something else they don't have. Yet all these things, far from producing happiness by themselves, more often occasion restlessness, guilt, anxiety, complexity. What then do people need in order to be happy? Ecclesiastes' answer is blunt: Nothing at all, because whatever a person has right now is all that's needed for happiness. Therefore "enjoy life…all your meaningless days. For this is your lot" (9:9).

The story is told of a man who received a nicely wrapped gift, which he found to be empty inside. With a cry of joy he exclaimed, "Nothing! Just what I've always wanted!" This man knew that happiness doesn't inhere in having or achieving anything in particular, but in an attitude of heart. Dr. Seuss's Grinch stole the presents of Christmas, but he couldn't steal the joy. Ecclesiastes is a deliberately bleak book because the author wants to turn us away from all those obvious and external things that we think will make us happy, in order to point us to the true secret of happiness, which he calls "a gift of God."

If the secret of happiness is a gift, does this mean that not everyone has it? No, it's a free gift available to all. Ecclesiastes even gives the gift a name, calling it our "lot" or portion. Do you have a portion in life? I certainly do. Everyone does. Accept it as a gift. If you can't be happy, be content. Having a portion in life and being content with it are the only requirements for happiness.

JOY AND GLADNESS

May all who seek you rejoice and be glad in you.

PSALM 70:4

By now you may have gathered that I make no division in this book between joy and happiness. In conversations about my experiment, people often insist that these two are quite different. I'm not so sure. When I'm joyful, I'm happy, and when I'm happy, I'm joyful. What could be plainer? Why should I want anything to do with a joy that isn't coupled with happiness, or with a kind of happiness that is without joy? Happiness without joy is shallow and transient because it's based on outward circumstances rather than an attitude of the heart. As for joy without happiness, it's a spiritualized lie.

The Bible does not separate joy and happiness and neither should we. Repeatedly Scripture mentions the two together: "There was joy and gladness among the Jews" (Esther 8:17); "Let us rejoice and be glad in his salvation" (Isaiah 25:9); "May those who delight in my vindication shout for joy and gladness" (Psalm 35:27). In modern English *gladness* may even be a better word than either *joy* or *happiness,* because it breaks down any perceived division between the two. Without doubt gladness both floods the heart and shines on the face. Couldn't we use more of this quality in our Christianity?

If a proper distinction can be made between joy and happiness, perhaps it's like that between faith and works. These two are not distinct in the sense that sometimes we have one and sometimes the other; rather, they're two aspects of the same reality. Joy tends to be felt on the inside, deep down, while happiness is a matter of mining joy to form it into useful articles. When a man and woman first fall in love, they experience great joy. Will they then take that joy and work it into a secure, happy relationship?

True, an inner joy exists that doesn't readily translate into outward happiness, but this is the bud of the flower rather than its fruit. According to Galatians 5:22, joy is a fruit of the Holy Spirit—a word indicating fullness, maturity, a visible and tangible product. Consider the other fruit of the Spirit and ask whether those qualities are interior or exterior or both. For example, can we imagine an inner self-control that produces no outward discipline? How about an inner gentleness that doesn't result in a gentle manner? Or what good is an interior love that has no measurable effect upon relationships? In the same way, an inner, ethereal joy that brings no gladness to oneself or to anyone else is not the joy of the Bible.

Happiness keeps joy honest. If the heart is joyful, let it tell our face. Before Jesus healed a paralytic He asked, "Which is easier: to say, 'Your sins are forgiven,' or to say, 'Get up and walk'?" (Matthew 9:5). Similarly we can ask about joy: Which is easier: to believe in it or to live it? The proof of the pudding is in the eating. In a whole person the inner and the outer spheres of life blend. Healthy spirituality seamlessly connects the two, continually opening channels between heaven and earth. Happiness is the way heavenly joy handles daily life in this world.

Joy may be nourished by many sources, from theological meditations to sensual experiences. I hear strains of music, someone hugs or touches me, a flock of geese flies overhead in the dusk—and mysteriously my mood lifts and lightens. Is this joy or is it happiness? Does it matter? What matters is that life is hard and I need to gratefully enjoy these sips from the cup of glory.

SOUL AND STRENGTH

Do not grieve, for the joy of the LORD is your strength.

NEHEMIAH 8:10

The people of Nehemiah's day had been listening for hours to the Bible as it was read aloud, and it made them sad to realize how far they fell short of Scripture's lofty standards. When Nehemiah announced, "Do not grieve, for the joy of the LORD is your strength," the effect was electrifying: "All the people went away to eat and drink, to send portions of food and to celebrate with great joy, because they now understood the words that had been made known to them" (8:12). Hurray!—they finally understood the Bible.

Many people today know their Bibles well but do not grasp its message of joy. The result is Christians who believe all the right things but who go around with long faces. Nehemiah's words remind us plainly that the joy of the Lord is not only a spiritual reality but a physical one. If the joy of the Lord is your strength and you aren't joyful, then it follows that you are weak. Real joy is felt in the body; it can even be tasted on the tongue. The joy of the heart pervades body, mind, and emotions, bringing lightness to the step, brightness to the eyes, clarity to the thoughts.

We tend to use the word *spiritual* as if it's somehow separate from the physical. How wrong this is! Christianity, with its clear emphasis on physical incarnation and bodily resurrection, repudiates this heresy. Yes, the spiritual is greater than the physical, but precisely because it includes the physical. The joy of the Lord is like a muscle, and like a muscle it can be moved, flexed, used to wield tools and weapons, to accomplish work. A muscle that isn't used will soon atrophy, and the same is true of a theological joy that doesn't translate into happy living.

Scripture does not commend disembodied virtue—the kind that means well but does not follow through. To be authentic, virtue must be fleshed out in the real world. Joy, more than an inner state, is a dynamic confluence of interior and exterior in such a way that the world—beginning with one's personal world, then flowing out to touch others—is transformed. Real joy cannot help but erupt into real life, and the outward manifestation of this is happiness. Happiness is realized joy.

Joy is like breathing: It's not enough to breathe in; one must also breathe out. In a word: Rejoice! Let your joy reverberate. Hug someone. Dance. Speak some inspiring words. Write a letter or a book. Don't just think about happiness—be happy! Joy yearns to be physically expressed, acted out, lived. Many Christians have invited Jesus into their heart but not into their soul or strength.

Unhappiness is not primarily a product of pain and hardship, but of resisting the will of God. For many this is a hard teaching. When crushed by suffering, it's cruel to be told that we ought to be happy. While it's true that seasons of bleakness may come and must simply run their course, still the gospel continually nudges us toward celebration. Anyone is welcome to resist this nudge, but no gladness will be found that way.

Besides being orthodox (having right doctrine), we must also be orthopathic, a word that means "having right feelings." Scripture exhorts us not just to believe the right things but to feel the right feelings. Again and again we're told, "Do not grieve," "Fear not," "Be content," "Do not worry," "Peace be with you." Taken together, these directives add up to a picture of happiness, of interior joy so worked into corporeal existence that the outcome is a happy life.

AUTHENTICITY

·

[Happy] are the poor in spirit,
for theirs is the kingdom of heaven.

MATTHEW 5:3

How can I tell when I'm in the kingdom of heaven? I'm happy about it! Jesus' Beatitudes promise clearly that happiness (or blessedness) is the result of a godly life. Often when Scripture uses the word *blessed,* it's possible to translate it (as some versions do) as *happy.* Jesus opens His Sermon on the Mount with a list of nine qualities—from meekness and mourning to persecution—that He guarantees will ensure happiness.

But wait: How can we explain the apparent contradiction in these statements? Consider Matthew 5:4—"[Happy] are those who mourn." Is it possible for the sad to be happy?

Throughout my experiment in joy I wrestled with this paradox. Could I "rejoice in the Lord always" and still acknowledge all the unhappy feelings that any normal person may legitimately experience? Is happiness compatible with sadness, longing, loneliness, frustration? Oddly, I discovered that the answer is yes. Indeed there can be no real happiness without a full range of all the other human emotions accompanying it. A rich, authentic humanity is the soil out of which joy grows.

This is the essence of Jesus' teaching in the Beatitudes. Happiness comes not to those who deny their weakness but to those who authentically inhabit the inherent paradox of the human condition. Conquering sin isn't a matter of sublimating negative impulses but of acknowledging frailty and living in humble dependence on God. The joyful person doesn't shrink from the truth about himself but embraces all of it.

Joy, being confident enough to swallow up all opposition, is afraid of nothing. The merciful are happy precisely because they aren't afraid of sin, either in themselves or others, and so are free to offer mercy. Peacemakers are happy because they aren't afraid of anger; if they were, they couldn't be effective at making peace.

Interestingly, there's no beatitude for joy. Jesus does not say, "Blessed are the joyful." Obviously the joyful are blessed already and know it. Yet within this knowledge lies a danger of complacency, as Luke's inverted version of the Beatitudes warns: "Woe to you who laugh now, for you will mourn and weep" (6:25). If I go around thinking I'm rich in spirit, I receive no blessing. The blessing is obtained through owning my poverty.

Happiness can be dangerous. From my experiment I know that too steady a focus on joy may actually lead to its opposite; inadvertently one begins to force good feelings, until eventually little room remains to breathe or be human. The qualities of the Beatitudes, however, are ones a human being can live and move with, day in and day out. These are the wellsprings of joy.

Significantly, the last beatitude—the blessing upon "those who are persecuted because of righteousness"—is the happiest one of all. To these people Jesus crows, "Rejoice and be glad, because great is your reward in heaven" (Matthew 5:12). Notice He doesn't say, "Just wait till you see how happy you'll be in heaven!" Rather He says, "Rejoice now, in the midst of your trouble, because you know your reward is coming." In this upside-down view, the greatest joy issues from the greatest worldly trouble.

Maybe we're looking for joy in the wrong places? The Beatitudes teach that happiness does not exist in isolation, but rather is the fruit of certain other godly qualities—humility, purity, peacemaking, courage. Pursue joy for its own sake, and anything that seems to go wrong comes as a grievous blow. But resolve to rejoice always and only in the Lord, and everything that goes right comes as a blessing.

THE BRIDEGROOM'S VOICE

The friend who attends the bridegroom waits and listens
for him, and is full of joy when he hears the bridegroom's voice.
That joy is mine, and it is now complete.

JOHN 3:29

J oy has a voice. People are unhappy because they listen to unhappy voices. If you're unhappy right now, it's certain that an unhappy voice is sounding in your mind. To become joyful you must listen to a joyful voice, distinguishing the one note of joy from all the other voices that clamor for attention.

No one in the universe is more miserable than Satan. The devil cannot give voice to true joy; it's impossible for him. He can tempt us in many ways, but he cannot tempt us by reproducing the voice of joy. All he can do is deceive us with a voice that, though not happy itself, seems to promise happiness.

The voice of the Lord, however, is the voice of joy itself. So much human misery, so much evil and restlessness and wasted time, could be avoided if we would only develop the habit of listening for the voice of joy and insist on following it and no other. Jesus said, "My sheep listen to my voice; I know them, and they follow me." He also said, "They will never follow a stranger; in fact, they will run away from him because they do not recognize a stranger's voice" (John 10:27,5).

In our pursuit of happiness, it isn't happiness alone we pursue but the God of happiness, the only one who can make us happy. If we want to be happy, we must listen to the Joy Giver and obey Him in all things. Since He intends for us to "go out in joy and be led forth in peace" (Isaiah 55:12), without happiness it's difficult even to hear what He's saying, let alone obey. His voice is the voice of joy.

Naturally anyone who makes a firm decision to walk in joy will face challenges. All kinds of forces will conspire to distract and pull one off balance. There will be war in the spirit, and the only way to win and restore peace is through discernment—correctly discerning the still, small, happy voice of the Lord and following Him only.

Most believers have a favorite Bible verse, one that has spoken to them again and again. Mine is James 3:17: "The wisdom that comes from heaven is first of all pure." In this passage James contrasts two kinds of wisdom—one motivated by "envy and selfish ambition" that produces "disorder and every evil practice," and the other characterized by purity and peace that produces "a harvest of righteousness." James simplifies things for us by pointing out that there are not many kinds of spiritual voices, but only these two. My life's work, I feel, has been distinguishing between these two voices, and learning to choose unerringly the one from heaven.

An experiment in joy is an experiment in listening to and following Jesus. If we make up our minds to follow Jesus in everything, often we won't know how to proceed. We must ask Him and listen for His answer. Before we can hear Him properly, we might have to slow down, get some rest, make some changes. Even then, when the answer we've been seeking does come, we may not be able to believe our ears. It will probably seem too simple to us, too undemanding, too good to be true.

This is the voice of joy. When God starts telling you things that are too good, so great and wonderful that you laugh out loud with joyous relief, you'll know you're in touch with the real Jesus.

BLESSINGS AND CURSES

Because you did not serve the LORD your God joyfully and gladly
in the time of prosperity, therefore in hunger and thirst,
in nakedness and dire poverty, you will serve
the enemies the LORD sends against you.

DEUTERONOMY 28:47-48

The Bible spells out clearly the way of joy. God wants the path to be so obvious that He once dramatized the difference between happiness and misery by dividing the Israelites into two groups and having them stand on two different mountains. From one mountaintop the people shouted out the curses that would come upon anyone who disobeyed the Lord, and from the opposite mountaintop rang out the blessings that would accompany obedience. Turn to Deuteronomy 28 now and read over the extravagant list of promised blessings. See if they don't knock your socks off. And just think: "All these blessings will come upon you and accompany you if you obey the LORD your God" (verse 2).

Later in the chapter, read of all the unhappiness that must surely overtake the disobedient: "The LORD will send on you curses, confusion and rebuke in everything you put your hand to, until you are destroyed" (verse 20). Is it fair for God to curse and destroy people? It's not a matter of fairness but of facing facts. If you want to drive safely, obey the rules of the road. Ignore traffic lights, and you'll soon be in a wreck.

Have these blessings and curses of Deuteronomy been discontinued? No, they stand as firm today as ever. The Lord doesn't issue rubber checks. He told His people plainly how to be happy, yet they turned a deaf ear, and so there came upon them all the curses they'd been warned of. The choice was clear—

blessings for obedience, curses for disobedience. Happiness or misery. Perhaps it's difficult for us today to see our own relationship to joy in such black-and-white terms, yet if we treat joy as a gray area, what color will our joy be?

There's a direct correlation between happiness and pleasing God. "To the man who pleases him, God gives wisdom, knowledge and happiness" (Ecclesiastes 2:26). Mary, who "found favor with God" (Luke 1:30), produced one of the Bible's great songs of joy: "My soul glorifies the Lord and my spirit rejoices in God my Savior" (Luke 1:46-47).

The Lord cares more about adverbs than verbs. He doesn't want us just to serve Him; He wants us to serve Him joyfully. Without joy, all our work and sacrifices, even our flawless theology, cannot please Him. God doesn't love a giver, He "loves a cheerful giver" (2 Corinthians 9:7). More than our money or our work, He wants us to be happy.

As a parent, would you be pleased with dutiful children who went around heavy-hearted, oppressed with guilt and anxiety, fearful of suffering consequences for their every misdeed and never lightening up enough to share a laugh or a relaxing moment with you? Don't loving parents want their children to enjoy life? "Which of you, if his son asks for bread, will give him a stone?" (Matthew 7:9).

Why aren't more Christians happy? Why is real joy so rare among us? Isn't it because we don't truly believe in a loving heavenly Father whose highest desire is for His children's happiness? Our joy is the reason behind everything He does. The message of Jesus' parable of the wedding banquet is that God invites us to a party, but no one wants to go! Our King has made us a joyful kingdom, and He's eager to see us delight in it. If we don't, if all we do is stand around frowning and griping, He might have to challenge us, as the king did a shabbily dressed guest at the wedding banquet: "How did you get in here without wedding clothes?" (Matthew 22:12).

A WINNING ATTITUDE

I consider that our present sufferings are not worth comparing
with the glory that will be revealed in us.

ROMANS 8:18

W hat attitude do you bring to your present sufferings? Can you
taste the glory to be won through them, or do you wish they'd
just go away? Wishing problems away is a sure recipe for bringing them on.
The devil smells this weakness in us, this reluctance to fight, and moves in
swiftly for the kill. It's much harder for him to attack those who, knowing
they'll emerge victorious, are willing to take on anything.

Once when I felt weak and defeated, a friend asked me, "Have you ever
lost a fight?" Immediately I saw what he meant: Every problem I'd ever had
was behind me, except for the one I now faced, and surely it too would go
down to the dust. My friend's question snapped me to my senses, and I
answered, "No, I've never lost."

In Christ our very defeats are the stuff of victory. The devil can never win
against us, because fighting Christians is like fighting a hydra: For every head
lopped off, two more sprout in its place. For every apparent triumph of darkness, a far greater victory is achieved for the faithful in the kingdom of
heaven. As Paul says, "Our light and momentary troubles are achieving for us
an eternal glory that far outweighs them all" (2 Corinthians 4:17).

It makes all the difference whether I see my problems as light and
momentary or as heavy and insoluble. Once I determine to take up my cross
and face each trial courageously, it becomes quite possible to live without
heaviness at all. Problems are only heavy if I'm not sure I can lick them.

Happy people have just as much pain as anyone else, in some cases more.

It could even be argued that the happy feel pain more acutely than the unhappy, whose feelings are relatively numb. The real difference in happy people is that they're not trapped by their pain. Rather than settling inside a happy soul, pain moves through it as through a channel, and that channel is joy. Joy keeps pain moving.

Happiness, rather than indicating an absence of pain, denotes a certain efficiency of processing life's problems. Happy people don't stay stuck for long; their lives are too rich for that. Greater happiness empowers them to take on more challenges, and moving through challenges makes them happier still.

Joy knows it's on the winning side. That's why it can rejoice even in the midst of suffering. If any of life's horrors were permanent or unconquerable, joy would be impossible. Yet how easily we're cowed into a defeatist attitude! It doesn't take a major calamity to get us down; a petty annoyance will do nicely. A day, an entire week, indeed a lifetime, can be spoiled by a series of light and momentary troubles. While one believer praises God in the midst of terminal illness, another grumbles because of a runny nose. What's the difference between these two lives? Attitude.

Take the attitude of a victim and you'll be crushed; adopt a winning attitude and you'll excel. The victim, faced with a problem, trembles and wishes the problem would go away. The victor, faced with the identical problem, looks it squarely in the eye and moves forward. A friend who battled cancer adopted this motto: "Cancer doesn't play fair; it plays to win—and so do I."

In the words of James Birrell, a boy who died of neuroblastoma at the age of eight, "You can't let cancer ruin your day."

SPIRITUAL WARFARE

Do not rejoice that the spirits submit to you,
but rejoice that your names are written in heaven.

LUKE 10:20

A book about joy is necessarily a book about spiritual warfare. What exactly is meant by this much-used term? Mostly it's a matter of attitude. "Take your stand against the devil's schemes," says Paul (Ephesians 6:11). There's a war going on and we're in it. God's warrior should be dressed and ready for battle at all times. The moment we lie down on the job, the battle's lost, for the enemy never rests.

Jesus knew that the great danger in spiritual warfare is to become preoccupied with the darkness. His disciples became so excited over all the demons they were driving out that He had to calm them down by reminding them of the true basis of joy. Spiritual triumphs may thrill, but joy rests in the simple fact that our "names are written in heaven." From this joy alone comes the strength to attack and defeat the enemy.

Life is an unrelenting war between good and evil. This is why we're here—to fight this war. This is the answer to the question "Why do bad things happen?" or "Why does God permit evil?" Evil is evil, but the war against it is good. To fight the good fight is the purpose of life. Anyone who fails to recognize and accept this basic fact will have a hard time finding joy.

Jesus Himself gave spiritual warfare first priority over all His other work. Immediately after His baptism He "was led by the Spirit into the desert to be tempted by the devil" (Matthew 4:1). Only after winning this initial battle could He take up His ministry "in the power of the Spirit" (Luke 4:14). Later Jesus taught that "no one can enter a strong man's house and carry off his

possessions unless he first ties up the strong man. Then he can rob his house"
(Mark 3:27).

Many of us try to accomplish work for the Lord without first subduing
the enemy. If we haven't robbed the enemy's house, then he'll rob ours, and
first to go will be our joy. If he succeeds in stealing our joy, everything else
goes with it. What good are all our blessings if we can't enjoy them? Conversely,
if the devil can't steal our joy, neither can he steal anything else of value.
There's no robbing a happy man.

If we want joy, we'll have to fight for it, deliberately and fiercely. In our
tame, airbrushed society it's all too easy to sleepwalk through life, falling prey
to monstrous evils lurking under a veneer of civility, material comfort, false
security. As our civilization crumbles from within, our attention is diverted by
selfish, shortsighted goals and petty complaints. Intentionally engaging in war
against the unseen foe clarifies the true nature of our struggles and tightens
our grip on reality.

If we aren't winning spiritual battles, we'll have little joy. A lazy and complacent happiness will soon dissipate. Joy doesn't just sit around enjoying
itself; when necessary it's aggressive, feisty, uncompromising. Joy brooks no
opposition. "As long as it is day," said Jesus, "we must do the work of him
who sent me" (John 9:4). That work was "to destroy the devil's work" (1 John
3:8). Are we about our Father's business? Are we triumphing daily over anger,
worry, doubt, lethargy?

Since spiritual warfare is not an option but a necessity, we might as well
be happy about it. Waging war in Christ's name is not an oppressive duty but
a royal privilege integrally linked to joy. Our Warrior God wants us to know
the pleasure not only of winning but of fighting itself. If we shrink from
struggles, we abdicate a part of our humanity. To be fully alive is to plow full-
steam into life, acknowledging all of it, horrors included. No joy has come to
me through denying evil, but only through embracing the charge given at my
Anglican baptism: "manfully to fight under Christ's banner against sin, the
world, and the devil, and to continue Christ's faithful soldier and servant
unto my life's end."[4]

LOVE THE STRUGGLE

Fight the good fight of the faith.

1 TIMOTHY 6:12

The secret of winning at spiritual warfare is to love it. One must love war the way soccer players love soccer, with a savage alacrity. One must love the battle itself, the surge of adrenaline, the feeling of strength and skill, the cries of the vanquished, the smell of blood.

Don't the demons, in their own way, love what they do? Surely they love attacking us. They also tremble in their boots, but something like love must drive them too. This is where we have the edge. In Christ we're motivated not just by something like love, but by love itself, which "drives out fear" (1 John 4:18). When we love war more than the enemy does, we cannot lose. Loving war is the way to win.

The devil knows a secret about people. He knows that most of us don't want trouble. We don't like it. When trouble comes we shy away, trying to act as if everything's cool. Most people will do almost anything to avoid confrontation. What holds us back from winning the battles of life is that, far from loving war, we view it as dirty work to be avoided at all costs. We'd rather do anything, even wash feet, than encounter what the Bible calls "the spiritual forces of evil in the heavenly realms" (Ephesians 6:12).

In the days of Samson, the Lord "was seeking an occasion to confront the Philistines" (Judges 14:4). As Christians we should cultivate this same attitude. Though we may not confront the powers of darkness directly, we can be certain that God will do this through us, and we must be ready. More than ready, we should be eager to engage the foe. Far from avoiding problems, we should be spoiling for a good scrap, knowing that through it the kingdom of

God will be advanced. While we don't love trouble for its own sake as the devil does, we smell the opportunity in it. We learn not to hate struggles but to love them because they're a chance to take action against the enemy and to expand the territory of our happiness.

Christians should love war for three reasons. First, we fight in the knowledge that Christ is our Commander and He is the one who wages war. We love war in His name and for His sake. Secondly, we love war because it's necessary; there is evil in the world and it must be combated. Thirdly, we love war because of its ultimate end or goal, which is peace. Though in worldly affairs we're peace lovers, in the spiritual realm we know that the path of peace is a warpath.

Can't we love the outcome without loving the process? No, because the process itself is also good. Spiritual war is a good thing; if it weren't, Jesus wouldn't want us doing it. He wants us to fight alongside Him. He longs for us to rise up out of our misery and apathy, to take arms against the foe, and to feel the joy of victory flowing in our veins. He wants us to know how real and alive we feel when, "struggling with all his energy" (Colossians 1:29), we oppose the things that oppress us.

Christ knows that rising up against the enemy of our souls is the only way we can be free. He'll supply the weapons, the courage, the power, and everything else—but only we can supply the will to fight. Only we can decide to love this work as much as God does, and so get on with it.

Do you love God's will? Then love to wage war. Jesus does. He gave His life in battle. He loves war because He loves us. If I had to choose one key to joy as being most important, it would be this: Love the struggle.

THE TASTE OF
VICTORY

Shouts of joy and victory resound in the tents of the righteous:
"The LORD's right hand has done mighty things!"
PSALM 118:15

Joy is integrally linked to struggle. Joy doesn't come from standing still
but from making progress against opposition. If joy rests, it does so
only to survey its conquests. The taste of victory is essential to joy, and to be
victorious one must have an opponent. Joy needs to feel itself pushing against
forces that are capable of destroying it. The greater the odds, the greater the
potential for joy.

When I pay close attention to what goes on inside me during the course
of an average day, I find few moments of pure happiness, few times that aren't
shadowed by some dark thought or emotion. As on a day of bright sunshine,
though the shadows do not predominate, I cannot deny their presence. More
often than not God prepares His "table before me in the presence of my enemies" (Psalm 23:5). To avert my gaze ever so slightly from the feast is to see
the enemies—doubt, apathy, fear—lurking around.

If joy is seldom experienced in perfect purity, this isn't to say the real
thing is rare. On the contrary, without resistance joy loses its edge and grows
complacent. God knows perfect happiness in Himself, but we know happiness only by contrast with unhappiness.

When I first told my ten-year-old daughter Heather that I intended to
write a book on joy, she looked worried. Immediately she sat down and wrote
me this note:

Dear Daddy:

Today you had the idea that you would write a book on joy. Since you are writing this book, you may become very unhappy, because the Devil won't want you to finish it. When you're feeling down, TAKE THIS NOTE AND READ IT!

Signed, Wise words from Heather.

Wise words indeed! Heather knew very well that a life of joy inevitably draws fire from the enemy. She knew also that if anyone becomes unhappy, it's not God's doing but the devil's. At the least sign of joy the enemy comes along and says, "So you're going to be happy, are you? I don't think so." And stretching out his little pitchfork, he jabs us somewhere, and before we know it, we're sick, our mood changes, a family argument arises, or some plan is dashed.

Such things are bound to happen. When they do, TAKE THIS BOOK AND READ IT! If nothing else, read Heather's note and heed the warning of a child. The devil will try to frighten us, but we needn't give in. In Christ we have the power to defeat him, and Jesus wants us to know the sweet taste of victory.

Battles in the Old Testament were against flesh-and-blood foes, but today the battleground has shifted. Jesus returned to heaven so that the Holy Spirit could come, and the Holy Spirit came so that the battle could move within. The Lord could have destroyed all of Israel's enemies Himself, without any- one else lifting a finger, but He wanted the Israelites to fight too and not be afraid. Why? Because the war is about not just defeating our enemy, but over- coming our fear. Our joy depends upon it.

How strange and vibrant and astounding is this gift of life! So what if it's hard? So what if we're hounded by troubles, pressured and embattled on all sides? So many good gifts outweigh the trials. Thank God that we encounter some resistance to our cavalier passage through this world. Thank God He has designed life not to be easy but to test us to the limit and so turn lazy ingrates into children of God who are strong and fearless and full of love.

STANDING OVATION

Let them sacrifice thank offerings
and tell of his works with songs of joy.

PSALM 107:22

When is it a sacrifice to offer thanks? When I don't feel like it. This marks the difference between thanksgiving and gratitude. Gratitude is an attitude of heart, whereas thanksgiving is an act. If the act of giving thanks is not performed, gratitude will not develop.

Years ago, realizing I needed to develop gratitude, I began the practice of saying thanks to God for five things every night before bed. I still do this whenever I feel the least bit low. Looking for reasons to be thankful, instead of focusing on worries or fears, is like putting on a new pair of glasses. Life looks different through the lens of thanks.

If you are so low that you have only one prayer to offer, let it be a prayer of thanks. It's the easiest way to pray and often the most powerful. Moreover there's an intimate connection between thanksgiving and joy. In some circumstances thanksgiving, like forgiveness, is both the quickest and the only route to joy. Prayers of thanks, offered from the heart, always draw one closer to the light and therefore to the fire of joy.

Giving thanks is a way of gathering joy. Imagine yourself in a meadow chasing butterflies with a net. Though the meadow is full of spiders, you don't notice these; neither are you concerned with weeds or scraps of litter. You aren't collecting spiders or weeds or litter. You're collecting butterflies, and your sole focus is on capturing those brightly colored flecks of beauty.

Joy requires single-mindedness. The world is full of reasons to be sad or distressed, but beauty and goodness also abound. Which to look at? What you see is what you get.

Now imagine yourself in a meadow gathering wildflowers—violets, let's say. There are other flowers in the meadow, but you have eyes only for the purple violets. When you're finished, do you have a fistful of stones or twigs or grasses? No, you have a bouquet of violets.

Every day joy waits to be gathered. Will you take the trouble to find it, cherish it, be grateful? Joy is like a stranger standing on your doorstep, and gratitude is the host who opens the door and says, "Do come in and make yourself at home." Without gratitude, joy stands forever just outside the heart, making gestures that go unnoticed.

A joyful experience isn't really ours until we call it to mind and give thanks for it. How many such experiences are lost on us every day because, living without reflection, we never take time to pray them through our door?

Is God less good to us on our bad days? No, He doesn't change. He's always awesome and loving. Doesn't He deserve for us to be happy? Isn't He worth celebrating? He tips the sky like a goblet of light over our heads; He dresses the continents in the satiny robes of the seas. If He'd done nothing else, wouldn't these feats alone be worth a continuous clap of joy?

Joy glorifies God. When we feel good, God looks good. Don't be half-hearted for God; give Him a standing ovation every day. It's what He's waiting for. It's what you're waiting for too. Your whole being waits to erupt into thunderous and unending praise. You won't be happy until you do. You won't be happy until your first waking thought is of the glory of being alive. You won't be happy until like a little child you can hardly wait to get out of bed and tiptoe downstairs to see what magic awaits you. You won't be happy until you forget your problems long enough to look up to heaven and be stunned into heartfelt thanks for a life overflowing with goodness.

POWER OF CHOICE

Though the fig tree does not bud and there are no grapes on the vines,
though the olive crop fails and the fields produce no food,
though there are no sheep in the pen and no cattle in the stalls,
yet I will rejoice in the LORD, I will be joyful in God my Savior.

HABAKKUK 3:17-18

Habakkuk teaches us that joy is not dependent on circumstances but can be embraced at the worst of times. Happiness doesn't just happen; it involves an act of will. "Choose for yourselves this day whom you will serve" (Joshua 24:15). Habakkuk shows us what this choice looks like in practice.

Not long into my experiment I had "one of those days"—a day packed with unexpected frustrations. I made it through still clinging to joy, but just barely. By midnight my joy was hanging by a thread. If one more thing happened, I told myself, I'd snap. Just then, as I climbed the wooden hill one last time before falling into bed, I noticed that our dog had had diarrhea all over the hall carpet. Surveying this catastrophe, I realized I was faced with a choice. I could choose to throw away my joy, or I could choose to clean up the mess willingly and happily. So stunningly clear were these two options that it was as though the door of choice had swung open in my heart, showing me the tremendous power resting in the decision of a moment.

Thankfully, that night I chose joy, and I went to bed as happy as I've ever been in my life.

Happiness is a choice. Rather, it's a series of choices, a series of steps taken one after another in the same direction. You, no matter where you are, can take one of these steps right now. The wounds in your heart will not be healed by a one-time miracle but by making small choices, one after another, to believe rather than doubt, to be happy instead of miserable. While suffering is inevitable, misery is optional. Pain cannot be avoided, but joy can. If you don't believe in the power of choice, you won't experience it.

Step One of the Twelve-Step Program reads, "We admitted we were powerless." A friend, confronted with this step at his first meeting, confessed to being powerless over lust. Two years and many meetings later, my friend still had a big problem with lust. As a recovering alcoholic with over twenty years of sobriety, I finally challenged him, "Why don't you just give it up? Lust is no different from drinking. It may seem easier to give up alcohol because it's a tangible thing, but the program works just as well for lust. You really can give it up."

The same is true of unhappiness. Misery is an addiction. To get free, one must make a clean break so that unhappiness is no longer an option. The first step, just as for the alcoholic or addict, is to acknowledge one's powerlessness over a wasting disease. Then, as the alcoholic cannot touch a drink, for the melancholic there can be no more trips to the unhappiness bar. Whenever a problem arises one must choose some other way besides woe-is-me to deal with it. This won't happen merely through reading a book, seeing a counselor, or attending some great conference. Rather, it happens by recognizing the door of choice in the center of one's will and stepping through it.

I haven't the slightest doubt that God is bending over backward all day long to give me joy—but I must take it. Jesus stands at the crossroads pointing the way to joy, inviting and encouraging, but I must choose. Lasting happiness comes only through choice, through the making of countless small decisions, one day at a time. Once I see this, it's not hard to choose. The hard part is admitting I have a choice.

CHANGING BELIEFS

May the righteous be glad and rejoice before God;
may they be happy and joyful.

PSALM 68:3

I'm convinced that the main obstacle to happiness is lack of faith. People are unhappy because they don't believe in happiness. They believe in same-old-same-old. To undertake my experiment in joy, I had to change beliefs. From a stick-in-the-mud theology of sadness I had to switch to a theology of happiness.

For years I believed it was a good thing to be sad. Sadness was compassionate, pragmatic, often the most realistic response to life's complexities. What a surprise to discover that a lingering, low-grade melancholy was actually my last line of defense against the love of God. Moodiness was how I got back at God for everything that had ever gone wrong in my life. Atheists get back at God by not believing in Him, but that option was closed to me. I couldn't help believing in God; the evidence was too compelling. I knew the world was filled with wonders, that life was precious beyond words, that I was surrounded by signs and messages of the power and love of my Creator. In view of all this, how could I justify clinging to my self-centered moodiness?

The answer was simple: Believe in sadness. Believe that a certain degree of melancholy is inevitable in this world. Believe that joy is brief and unsustainable, the rare exception rather than the rule. A capricious blessing, not a commandment.

Are you unhappy today? Ask yourself what you believe. What is your excuse for believing you cannot live this day in joy? No one can be happy without believing that happiness is good, right, appropriate, and allowed. If we believe joy is in short supply and must be carefully rationed, we will not rejoice. The lavish abundance of God's kingdom isn't obvious to the naked eye; it can be enjoyed only by those who believe, with a faith intense enough to lead to action.

Faith and works go hand in hand. Anyone who truly believes in the kingdom of heaven will work to usher it in. We will not work for what we do not believe in, and this principle applies to happiness. Not believing in it, we won't lift a finger to make it happen. Fundraisers are familiar with the idea of the matching grant, by which a wealthy donor promises to give a dollar (or sometimes a larger lump sum) for every dollar raised by the designated charity. God operates in a similar way. He knows we cannot afford joy, and He wants to give it to us freely, but first He requires a show of willingness. For every step of faith we take in this direction, He rewards us handsomely so that gradually we have more and more of what we couldn't possibly obtain on our own.

How might our actions change if we changed our beliefs about happiness? Consider the man who despises his job. What would happen if he believed, truly, that he could be happy in his work, either in his present job or in an entirely new career? Believing this, he would start to move toward this goal. He would make changes, he would dare to act differently, he would sacrifice, he would do whatever it took to follow his dream. Instead of feeling trapped in the belief that there's no way to be happily employed, now he would believe that there must be a way, and he would keep on seeking until he found it. And so he would become the beneficiary of Jesus' promise "Seek and you will find" (Luke 11:9).

COMMITMENT

Let all who take refuge in you be glad;

let them ever sing for joy.

PSALM 5:11

I f you were given the chance to be happy for the rest of your life, wouldn't you jump at it? I believe the Bible does make this offer, yet most of us hang back, reluctant to endure another wound of disappointment. Surveying the ninety days of my experiment, I see how often I went astray by compromising my original daring goal. I see also how the Lord kept calling me back to the pure and simple premise that yes, He does want His children to live in joy, and there's a way to do it if we'll trust Him.

The way begins with commitment. To become a Christian in the first place, one decides to follow Jesus no matter what. Why not make a similar commitment in regard to joy—to rejoice in the Lord always, no matter what? Isn't it only lack of faith that keeps us from this?

In conversations I've given up on trying to argue people out of their unhappiness. The more one reasons with them, the more their eyes glaze over. Theologically most Christians will probably agree that the Bible teaches and offers a life of joy, yet deep down they're not convinced. They're especially not convinced that such a life is possible for them, or for any ordinary person, right now. Neither seeing nor believing in the joy set before them, they're resigned to unhappiness, and so that's what they get.

Resignation is a form of commitment. In effect these skeptics are committed to their own unhappiness. Some may not admit they're unhappy, yet neither can they claim to be deeply happy. They've stopped short of abundant joy, the achieving of which requires a determination to leave none of joy's stones unturned. Happy times may come to anyone haphazardly, but if happiness is to be part of the character, one must resolutely take hold of it. One must choose joy, and keep on choosing it under all conditions, until gradually it becomes a habit, a self-sustaining reality. Lives change not through having some colossal experience but rather by making small, hard, daily choices.

In the same way that a commitment to love erodes selfishness, a commitment to joy provides a place to stand against all worldly vicissitudes. Do you want to live in fear, always wondering if some calamity will ruin your life? Then remain committed to the notion that it's impossible to rejoice in all circumstances. But if you want to be free, commit to joy come what may. In view of all that can happen to foil happiness, resolve deep within, "Nothing will stop me. I'm fixing my eyes on Jesus, and I'm not letting anything interrupt my joy in Him."

Something happens in the face of such a decision. When every option to be gloomy is removed, a profound shift takes place in the soul. Where before there seemed no way ahead, suddenly a path appears. An act of commitment is like having a flashlight in a dark forest. No longer is one blind and lost, for commitment itself lights the way. All the power of heaven is released to help the one who is firmly resolved to unlock its secrets. When I dedicated myself to ninety days of joy, I was amazed at how God began to lavish His joy upon me in the most surprising ways. By myself I couldn't possibly engineer a joyous life, but when in faith I took joy's hand, joy did the rest.

Paul wrote, "Let the peace of Christ rule in your hearts" (Colossians 3:15). So with joy. You cannot control joy, but you can give joy permission to control you. Let joy take over your life and it will.

THE TRUE GOSPEL

Even though you do not see him now,
you believe in him and are filled
with an inexpressible and glorious joy.

1 PETER 1:8

Wherever there is true faith in Jesus, there is joy. When considering the claims of different versions of Christianity with their various theologies and lifestyles, look for the identifying mark of joy. Don't accept any gospel without it.

The New Testament is full of warnings against making any twists or additions to the gospel. The apostles were passionately concerned with preserving the vitality of the original message. They were devoted to separating the true gospel from anything that threatened to water down or taint its power. Paul felt this so strongly that he wrote, "Even if we or an angel from heaven should preach a gospel other than the one we preached to you, let him be eternally condemned!" (Galatians 1:8).

The true gospel is Jesus, just to know whom is to be "filled with an inexpressible and glorious joy." Joy is the presence of Someone who comes alongside and says, "Peace be with you," "Your sins are forgiven," "My burden is light," "Be of good cheer." Are you hearing Jesus speak these words to you? If you're not hearing and believing them, you don't know the gospel. No wonder you're unhappy!

According to Peter, Christian joy causes one to "greatly rejoice" even if "now for a little while you may have had to suffer grief in all kinds of trials" (1 Peter 1:6). Peter concludes, "This is the true grace of God. Stand fast in it" (5:12). In order to experience the true gospel, it's necessary to "stand fast"—

an expression that appears in the New Testament more than a dozen times. Why are we so easily swayed, so easily persuaded to accept a version of the gospel (and therefore a quality of life) without real joy? What would it take for us to stand up for ourselves and insist on our rights?

Those who know the gospel "do not lose heart," for "though outwardly we are wasting away, yet inwardly we are being renewed day by day" (2 Corinthians 4:16). Have you been renewed today, or are you losing heart? Yesterday's joy will not do for today. Each day we need a fresh anointing. Each day we need to be renewed by receiving the good news of the gospel all over again.

Many times Paul referred to his message as "my gospel." It was a message for everyone, but it was also something revealed to him alone, something he'd discovered for himself. Have you discovered the gospel for yourself? Do you know *your* gospel? You cannot have anyone else's faith; you can only have your own. The verses, prayers, disciplines, and good advice that have worked for someone else may not work for you. The Bible's message is tailor-made for you, perfectly designed to fit your need. You'll know this good news by the fact that it actually works to make you happy. It's so vibrant and exciting that it will renew your soul day after day.

Insist on the one authentic gospel of Jesus Christ, the "good news of great joy" (Luke 2:10). Accept no substitute. Why settle for a religion that doesn't lift your heart and set you to singing? Look for the gospel that has your own name stamped on it in pure gold.

WHO AM I?

The boundary lines have fallen for me in pleasant places;
surely I have a delightful inheritance.

PSALM 16:6

Some years ago I found myself reciting a litany of my weaknesses to a friend. "I don't do this well, I'm not good at that," and so on. Finally this man said, "You've just told me who you're not. Now tell me who you are."

At the time I blundered through a lame response, so lame that for years afterward I was haunted by this question: Who am I? I had to admit I didn't know. The question goaded me into a deeper and deeper search, until eventually the outlines of an answer began to emerge. As the answer grew in clarity, so did my joy. I see now that joy rests in a solid sense of identity. It depends upon knowing who I am, knowing that the "boundary lines" of my God-given temperament and gifts "have fallen for me in pleasant places."

To accept and live within my limitations is freeing. What a great sigh of relief is heard as false pressures and obligations are dropped. Not any false self, but only the true "I" can enter into the kingdom of heaven. All the phony must be left behind. To be faithful to my true self, I must continually resist not just sin but many forms of virtue that may not be appropriate for me right now, many legitimate expressions of Christianity that aren't legitimate for me, many good deeds that aren't mine to do. Christ's "narrow road" is that of doing only those acts that arise from real faith, knowing that "everything that does not come from faith is sin" (Romans 14:23).

A life of joy rests upon the discovery of what I, and I alone, am meant to do and then doing it with all my heart. As I glimpse the mystery of who I am, my road may indeed seem narrow, and as I press further on, it may grow so narrow that the decision to keep moving in this direction can be exceedingly difficult. Enormous forces will contend to distract me, to swerve me from the path of what I'm called to do and how I'm to do it. Joy depends upon narrowing and narrowing my peculiar destiny, clarifying and honing it to a gleaming point until all my energies are focused, like the rays of the sun through a magnifying glass, upon the accomplishment of my own unique purpose, the mystery of who I am.

God doesn't love who I'm not; He loves me. The evil one whispers, "Just being you is not enough; it's more complex than that." But God created me to be myself—the true self, formed in His image—nothing more nor less. Only I can love God; all that is not me must fall away. Leaving everything else behind, I must turn and follow Jesus in the nakedness of who I am, insisting, "I am enough, I do enough, I'm good enough." Loving myself as I am, I shall also love God as He is. In the words of Brent Curtis, "Let people feel the weight of who you are, and let them deal with it."[5]

Who am I? I may not know until that point when I see the whole world, perhaps even the whole church, moving in one direction, while I stop, turn, and without casting a glance over my shoulder, deliberately go the other way—perhaps not entirely understanding what I'm doing, but knowing that I'm following my Lord. This, if I can embrace it with all my heart, is the way of pure joy.

DELIGHT YOURSELF

Let Israel rejoice in their Maker;
let the people of Zion be glad in their King....
For the LORD takes delight in his people.

It's hard to like someone who doesn't return the favor. In order to rejoice in the Lord, it helps to know that He also rejoices in us. More than just rejoicing, He *delights* in us. *Delight* is a good, honest word that circumvents any phony spiritualizing of the word *rejoice*. If we rejoice in the Lord for theological reasons rather than with frank warm-heartedness, we'll presume that He's the same way—rejoicing in His people out of covenantal obligation, while in His heart barely able to tolerate our waywardness. How absurd! When the Bible says "The Lord takes delight in his people," we should picture a big, sloppy smile on God's face and fireworks going off around His throne—all for you and me!

Psalm 37:4 reads, "Delight yourself in the LORD and he will give you the desires of your heart." How interesting that it doesn't say "Delight in the Lord" but "Delight *yourself* in the Lord." One doesn't take joy in someone or something else without finding joy in oneself. The very expression "take joy" suggests that we receive as much as we give. Delighting in the Lord is fun; we should be having a ball!

The great struggle in this world is not between believers and unbelievers, but between two different kinds of belief—that which delights in God because He delights in us, and that which delights not. The distinguishing mark of true belief is delight.

What keeps us from having a good time with God? Mostly our own negative self-image—the very obstacle the gospel is meant to overcome. The previous chapter contained this sentence: "I am enough, I do enough, I'm good enough." To the extent that I cannot believe this of myself, I'll unconsciously project the same inadequate image onto God. Unbelievers do just this, feeling that even if God exists, He's not enough for them, He doesn't do enough, He's not good enough. When Christians believe they aren't good enough for God, it follows that they believe He's not good enough for them. While their theology tells them God is awesome and loving, in practice they feel that all His power and love haven't worked for them. They feel the gospel has failed them, when the truth is they just haven't believed it. To believe the good news is to know that in Christ I'm wholly righteous, good enough for God and also for me.

Negative self-talk is a powerful enemy of joy. We may think we're being humble or honest when actually we're tearing ourselves down, and God and others with us. At every point where we doubt ourselves, we really doubt our Lord. Thoughts that come from God possess a quality of light and joy that sets them apart from all other thoughts. If we don't find our lives imbued with these qualities, it's because, whatever our theology, we're thinking and believing lies.

In the same passage where Paul exhorts, "Rejoice in the Lord always," he teaches the kind of thinking that leads to joy: "Whatever is true, whatever is noble, whatever is right, whatever is pure, whatever is lovely, whatever is admirable—if anything is excellent or praiseworthy—think about such things" (Philippians 4:8). Think right now of something lovely or beautiful—a precious memory, a cherished dream, or perhaps just the light shining this moment on some ordinary object. Now open your heart and let that light in. Thank and worship your Creator for it. Don't let guilt and worry rule your mind. Instead let this one small beautiful thought fill your gaze. Let it be the spark that kindles delight in your soul.

RIVER OF DELIGHT

There is a river whose streams make glad the city of God.

PSALM 46:4

Sometimes I feel like an electric car. My batteries run down and I can't do anything until I get myself recharged. For me the process of recharging usually means sitting silently before the Lord for an hour or so and letting Him pour His Spirit into me.

During this time I have scant idea of how to pray or even how to think. I cannot seem to meditate or formulate coherent prayers, and whatever thoughts run through my mind are irrelevant. All that happens is that I feel a steady stream of God's love flowing into my spirit. I can literally feel myself being filled up.

I never know how long this process will take, and often it happens at times when I'm impatient to get on with some other business, or at least to pray in a more rational way. Instead I must be still and empty before the Lord, and I dare not move until the process is over. When it's finished, I know it, and then I emerge full of life and joy. However, if I try to end this mysterious work prematurely, or if I try to control it in any way, I always suffer. Either I don't have enough energy for the challenges that lie ahead, or else I'm immediately embroiled in some ugly spiritual battle that knocks me sideways.

In this book I'm simply reporting the results of an experiment. During my ninety days, over and over I found the Lord gloriously restoring my joy through the means I have just described, without me apparently contributing anything. Whenever this happened, I was strongly reminded that my experiment in joy was the Lord's idea, not mine. It was all the result of His initiative, and whatever joy I experienced came directly from Him.

Many readers will recognize what I've described as a form of contemplative prayer. For many years the Lord called me to this kind of prayer, while I remained resistant and skeptical. I stubbornly refused to comprehend that prayer could actually be worthwhile if I didn't "do" anything and if words, images, and thoughts formed no part of it.

Surely it's no coincidence that contemplative prayer finally caught up with me around the time of my experiment in joy. Suddenly it became clear that to live in joy I had to submit to these strange times of bathing in God's river of delight. As I did so, joy flowed naturally through my life. If I fought the process, the opposite happened, and joy eluded me.

Recent years have seen an upsurge of interest in contemplative prayer. Still, in many Christian circles this subject is hardly mentioned, and I wonder how commonly it's practiced. Is this, perhaps, one reason we have so little joy?

I'm not suggesting that everyone should pray exactly as I do. Nevertheless, to live in joy everyone must practice Proverbs 3:5—"Trust in the LORD with all your heart and lean not on your own understanding." Each individual must discover the way of relying less on human understanding and more and more on the pure inspiration of the Holy Spirit.

When Ezekiel came in a vision to the river of life, he first waded into it ankle-deep, then knee-deep, then up to his waist. Finally he found "it was a river that I could not cross, because the water had risen and was deep enough to swim in" (47:5). The Christian life begins with baptism, a dunk in the river, but it doesn't stop there. We're meant to stay wet.

COMPLETE JOY

I have told you this so that my joy may be in you
and that your joy may be complete.

JOHN 15:11

Joy is not halfhearted; completeness is one of its marks. Indeed completeness marks every good gift from above. Why be partly free if I can be "free indeed" (John 8:36)? Why be content with a little righteousness when I can share "the righteousness of God" (2 Corinthians 5:21)? Similarly, complete joy is ours for the asking. "Ask and you will receive," Jesus said, "and your joy will be complete" (John 16:24).

When I was a boy back in the 1950s, margarine came in clear plastic bags. White like lard, it contained a bubble of intense reddish-orange dye. To color the margarine yellow, one broke the dye bubble and kneaded the bag until the color spread all through. This was always my job. If I didn't get to do it, I was upset. I loved breaking that bubble and seeing the gradual transformation in the margarine, like a sunrise in a bag.

This is how the Lord works with us to spread joy throughout our beings. Jesus compared the kingdom of heaven to "yeast that a woman took and mixed into a large amount of flour until it worked all through the dough" (Luke 13:21). How often I've sat down to pray feeling spent and discouraged and twenty minutes later—or sometimes one minute later—felt completely refreshed. The change began with a pinch of yeast, with one ray of divine light, with the Lord's joy like a bubble of color bursting gently within me and radiating throughout soul and body.

That's how this book began. Three months before I started my experiment I went on a holiday with my family, tenting at Green Lake in the interior of

British Columbia. Green Lake never has mosquitoes in August, but this year there were more than I've ever seen anywhere. Moreover, it rained and rained. One night, filled with gloom, I lay awake in my sleeping bag listening to the pelting rain, having wet and itchy thoughts, and feebly praying. Were we about to set a new record for the worst holiday ever?

When I awoke in the morning, the first thing I noticed was the sun shining with a buttery glow through the green translucence of the tent. That warm glow touched me, and then it began to fill me. It came right into my mind, into my heart, into all my muscles and down into the soles of my feet. For about an hour, while my family slept, I lay perfectly still and basked in the warm sunshine of the Holy Spirit.

The next morning this happened again, and the next, and the next. All through our holiday and on into the fall the Lord kept coming to me first thing in the morning as I lay in bed. Our holiday that year was the best ever, and before I knew it I was launching an experiment in joy. I became willing to bet that the Lord would keep on refreshing me in this way—not always early in the morning, and not always so dramatically, but still in a perceptible way every day. Something new had come into me, a new trust, a new ability to relax and to go with the flow of each day's events. So profound was this change that I felt I had undergone a transformation in character.

I realize now that this "something new" was a gift the Lord had been wanting to give me all along, ever since I first became a Christian—the gift of complete joy. Finally I was ready to receive it. My joy, no doubt, is not as complete as that of some saints, but it's complete enough to delight and thrill me every day. It's as much as I can practically hold, and it keeps increasing.

OIL OF GLADNESS

The LORD has anointed me to preach good news to the poor.

He has sent me…to bestow on them

a crown of beauty instead of ashes,

the oil of gladness instead of mourning,

and a garment of praise instead of a spirit of despair.

ISAIAH 61:1,3

As a new father I felt insecure and impatient about looking after my infant daughter. I wanted to love and care for her, but I wanted other things more—to read, write, pray, and generally pursue my own selfish idea of the Christian life. One day, all alone with my little girl and feeling trapped, suddenly out of the blue and for no apparent reason, the joy of the Holy Spirit touched the top of my head and began to radiate throughout my body. It was exactly like a cup of warm oil being poured over my head and flowing all through me from head to toe. After this I felt completely free to enjoy my daughter and to lavish her with loving attention.

This is an example of what Isaiah calls "the oil of gladness." This is the "milk and honey" of the Promised Land. At the time I called this my "baptism in the Spirit," though now I suspect it wasn't my first such experience, only the first time I became so acutely aware of the Holy Spirit's unction. Gradually I've come to understand that the phenomenon of anointing is so common for every true disciple that it's no exaggeration to say that it happens every day. It certainly does for me. We're meant to live this way, full of the Spirit, filled daily like jars with the oil of His joy.

In the previous chapter I described the change of character I experienced just prior to beginning my experiment in joy—a change that came with trust in the Holy Spirit. I also noted that this change had actually begun much earlier, when I first became a Christian and was filled with the Spirit. The baptism of the Spirit, I now believe, coincides with conversion. This must be so because the knowledge that Jesus is the Son of God who forgives our sins is a revelation that can come only through the Holy Spirit.

Few new converts, however, fully grasp this fact. In many churches direct experience of the Third Person of the Trinity is not well understood, and teaching on the subject is murky. It can take years for a new Christian to become acquainted enough with the Spirit's ways to assimilate His work into daily life. The experience described above occurred when I'd been a Christian for about seven years, and twelve more years passed before I gained enough courage to launch my experiment in joy. While I had countless spiritual experiences in the intervening time, I was too dull to fit them all together into a working picture of the Holy Spirit as a Person, let alone to be His reliable vessel. The beginning of my experiment coincided with my realization that the Spirit's joy—His oil of gladness and garment of praise—could be mine every day.

The joy that comes through the Holy Spirit is the Lord's joy, not mine. I'm not talking merely about the satisfaction of overcoming some problem, but about the joy of the Lord Jesus who has once and for all overcome the whole world. This is the joy of someone raised from the dead and sitting at the right hand of God in heaven, for whom the battles of earth are all over. In this joy, by the miracle of faith, I share. In touch with this reality, whenever I encountered struggles and failures in my experiment, far from discouraging me they only awakened a hunger for a still deeper and more pervasive joy, running and spilling like warm oil into all the empty crevices of my being, into the very places of my failure.

PASS IT ON

We write this to make our joy complete.

1 JOHN 1:4

Like John in the verse above, I too write my book with this motive—to complete my joy by sharing it. Happiness, oddly enough, can be a lonely business, because so few people share one's joy. I know hardly anyone who strikes me as deeply happy, yet I know many, many who are stressed, bewildered, sad, or depressed. Many are sad without even knowing it.

I write this book as an attempt, in some small way, to change this picture. I want people to read my book and to grow more and more joyful with every page, just as I have done in writing it. In a sense I want to demystify joy, to make it common fare for every Christian. I want people to see that happiness is taught in the Bible and that God wants us to have it, starting now, and that the deep joy of living, far from being fickle, can be counted on to grow and expand and become purer and sweeter.

Like John I want my joy to come full circle by connecting with others. I know my joy is not complete until I have shared it, until others are happy along with me and for the same reasons. This is a biblical principle. Paul wrote to the Philippians, "Make my joy complete by being like-minded, having the same love, being one in spirit and purpose" (2:2). John, not content just to write about joy, longed to share his joy in person: "I hope to visit you and talk with you face to face, so that our joy may be complete" (2 John 12). Joy longs to share itself, to spill its banks and flood the whole world.

This morning someone in my neighborhood committed suicide. Having flirted with thoughts of suicide myself in former years, I know the pull that such a death exerts on other lives. Suicides tend to come in rashes. Everyone feels the tug of the spirit of despair that was powerful enough to suck a life prematurely out of the world.

Joy too has a potent effect. It's contagious. If one person can break free of the world's shackles and lay hold of joy, a powerful invitation is issued to everyone else. Here's an influence the opposite of suicide—someone bent on living life to the full.

What keeps us from abundant life? Why are we so sad? As I look into the eyes of all the sad ones around me, what I see most is the desire to be understood, to be heard, to be embraced, to be accepted just as one is. In a word, to be forgiven.

Forgiven for what? For being so miserable, I suppose. What a vicious circle! People cannot be happy, it seems, until their unhappiness has been entirely accepted and absorbed by someone else. How is this possible? Who can do this for them? Who would be so foolish as to embrace happily someone else's misery?

Only Jesus. And those who are filled with His Spirit. This is what Jesus came for, and this is what drove the Pharisees crazy—the way He'd look at a sick, paralyzed man who could do nothing for himself and say, "Son, your sins are forgiven.... Get up, take your mat and go home" (Mark 2:5,11). No counseling session, no ritual of repentance, not even a prayer—but in one second Jesus raises this man from total paralysis to full, energetic life.

He does the same today. He continues to say, not just to the physically sick but to the emotionally lame and broken, "I understand your unhappiness, and I accept you. Now leave your misery and get up and rejoice!" To the extent that you and I do the work of Jesus, conveying afresh His heart to those around us, our joy will be complete.

DISCERNMENT

Praise be to the LORD my Rock,
who trains my hands for war, my fingers for battle.

PSALM 144:1

The challenges to our happiness come from three different fronts—the world, the flesh, and the devil. The strategy for dealing with each is different: We must resist the devil, crucify the flesh, and stop loving the world. Confusion can arise from assuming we're under fire in one area when really the attack is in another. We can be crucifying the flesh when we should be resisting the devil, or vice versa. We can be trying to humble ourselves when we should be taking initiative.

Most of the battles I faced during my experiment (and there were plenty) came down to a matter of discernment: What approach or strategy to employ, what weapon to use? When a dispute arose with an acquaintance, for example, at first I tried to handle it with humble love and prayers of blessing. Strangely, the problem did not yield to this strategy, but returned day after day to haunt me. Then my eye happened to fall on these words from Psalm 140:9: "Let the heads of those who surround me be covered with the trouble their lips have caused." Finding many such passages in Psalms, almost against my will I began to pray in this bold fashion, and I was amazed at how quickly my problem vanished and joy took over.

Sometimes when my back is against the wall, I'll imagine myself jumping on a white horse and riding full tilt into the thick of my enemies, brandishing a bright sword and yelling bloodcurdling war whoops, ecstatically bent on mowing down everything in my path. If I must go to war, I might as well do it with savage exuberance.

As a boy I played with toy soldiers, enacting mock battles that to me were very real. As an adult, is it foolish to keep up this ruse, imagining myself a real warrior riding a horse and flailing a sword? Not at all. If I let the battles of life be abstract, I'm left disorganized and bewildered. The war is real, and I need real images to help me to fight well. Paul thought the same when he wrote his famous charge to "put on the full armor of God" complete with breastplate, helmet, shield, and "the sword of the Spirit" (Ephesians 6:11-18).

One night during my experiment, overcome by an encroaching lethargy, I went to bed swamped by feelings of insecurity and fear. Though I slept well, in the morning the same mood threatened. But this time I deliberately mounted my white horse and attacked the forces of evil surrounding me.

Nothing seemed to happen. I didn't sense any great victory or sudden change of mood. Nevertheless, by an act of will I made up my mind not to give in to defeat, just as Paul exhorts in Ephesians 6:13—"that when the day of evil comes, you may be able to stand your ground, and after you have done everything, to stand."

Now here's how the Lord works: Ten minutes later my neighbor phoned to ask if I could watch her seven-year-old daughter Emily for half an hour before school. At the end of that time, Emily gave me a hug, and with that hug from a little child, joy returned to me full strength, and I was happy for the rest of the day.

In spiritual warfare, while it's vital to discern the enemy's tactics and to employ our weapons appropriately, victory does not come from cleverness, from force of will, or from performing some ritual or technique, but from the Lord. "It is not by sword or spear that the LORD saves; for the battle is the LORD's" (1 Samuel 17:47). When I've done everything I can to resist the foe, joy issues from seeing the Lord rush sovereignly and spectacularly to my defense.

THE PROMISED LAND

To him who overcomes, I will give the right to eat
from the tree of life, which is in the paradise of God.

REVELATION 2:7

For years I've been fascinated by the seven letters that comprise chapters 2 and 3 of Revelation. I'm especially intrigued by the promises and gifts with which each letter closes. "To him who overcomes," goes the constant refrain, "I will give…" The gifts include manna, the morning star, a new name, white clothes, fruit from the tree of life. Who wouldn't be overjoyed with such gifts?

Clearly what's being offered is a taste of heaven. This is what joy is—a true taste, even in this life, of paradise. When Adam and Eve sinned, the way to the tree of life was closed, but now it's open again "to him who overcomes." Happiness is the result of overcoming the world by faith and so taking up residence now in the kingdom of heaven. Listen to Colossians 3:1-3: "Since, then, you have been raised with Christ, set your hearts on things above, where Christ is seated at the right hand of God. Set your minds on things above, not on earthly things. For you died, and your life is now hidden with Christ in God."

The problems that keep us from joy are "earthly things" that can be resolved only by looking to heaven. Joy is spiritual; the human mind alone is incapable of producing it. A decision to live in joy is a decision to overcome every earthly problem by the power of heaven. Since we have this power inside us in the form of the Holy Spirit, who is God Himself, there's no reason to settle for the world's agenda. Every compromise with the world is a stench in the spotless house of joy.

In the Old Testament God gave the Promised Land to the people of Israel, but they also had to take it, crossing over the Jordan River and claiming the land in faith. In the same way God will give us all the happiness we can hold, but we must also take it. We must wrest it from the powers of darkness by dint of courage, faith, struggle, warfare. The Promised Land isn't some big empty green pasture waiting for us to romp into it. The whole problem is that it's occupied by enemies. The place in the sun that is rightfully ours, through God's gift, is crawling with squatters and intruders, forces who would rather kill us than look at us. God is calling for stout-hearted warriors to oppose these enemies. Joshua was such a warrior, but after he died there were still foes left in the land because the Lord wanted "to teach warfare to the descendants of the Israelites who had not had previous battle experience" (Judges 3:2).

Often we act like God's victims instead of His warriors, His frail invalids instead of His exuberant kids. Our Father wants His children to stand up and claim what is ours. Conflict is a part of life; it's a given. If we're to remain happy, far from avoiding conflict we must choose it. In the words of a popular motto, "If you can't get out of it, get into it." Life is only unhappy for those who are caught napping. Deliberately facing conflict drastically reduces the odds of nasty surprises. A new struggle comes along and immediately we rise to meet it. We've developed a habit, a reflex for taking problems in stride. Through our mounting an offensive, suddenly the tables are turned so that our enemies do the struggling while we mop up.

Happiness isn't lowered to us on a silver platter from above. Enough comes that way to create a taste, a longing, but if we want to enter the Promised Land of joy, we must boldly take the initiative to be overcomers.

OVERCOMING FEAR

Be strong and courageous. Do not be terrified;
do not be discouraged.

JOSHUA 1:9

The greatest enemy of joy is fear. The quickest way to send your joy packing is to become afraid that it will leave or that something will happen to take it away. What a pitiful way to live! Nothing can be deeply enjoyed for fear it will soon be gone. Paradoxically, however, the way to hold on to joy is not to cling to it. When trouble arises and I say, "Oh no, my joy is gone!"—then it will be gone. If instead I relax my grip on joy and release it to adversity, accepting whatever life may bring, then nothing can intimidate me and steal my joy. Joy dwells in an open hand.

What are we so afraid of? Fundamentally our fear is not just of losing battles but of having to fight at all. Overcome the reluctance to fight, and the fear of losing dissipates. We must fight anyway, whether we like it or not. Far better to fight not with reality itself but with our real enemy. Author Roald Dahl, describing his combat experience in World War II, observed, "The only way to conduct oneself in a situation where bombs rained down and bullets whipped past was to accept the dangers and all the consequences as calmly as possible. Fretting and sweating about it all was not going to help."[6]

In Franklin Roosevelt's famous words, "The only thing we have to fear is fear itself." As it turns out, I don't really have to fight the devil at all; I only need to assume the right posture toward him. When I show him I mean business, my position dramatically changes. Look at the enemy with the fire of Christ in my eyes and immediately he flees.

As Israel under Joshua moved deep into Canaan to take possession of the

Promised Land, five cities and their kings formed an alliance to attack them. In one day this massive force was completely destroyed because "the LORD threw them into confusion before Israel" and "hurled large hailstones down on them from the sky" (Joshua 10:10-11). For the crowning touch, Joshua summoned the five defeated kings and had them lie prostrate on the ground. With all Israel gathered around, he told his army commanders, "Come here and put your feet on the necks of these kings" (verse 24). Then "Joshua struck and killed the kings and hung them on five trees" (verse 26).

Killing these kings wasn't the main point. The main point was for Israel's leaders to stand towering over their royal enemies and feel through the soles of their sandals the fragile spinal cords of these once-powerful men. Joshua wanted his people to have this feeling in the balls of their feet and never to forget it.

Imagine this feeling now. Imagine you're in a position to crush your worst enemies as they cower before you—not human beings, but the dark, invisible powers that dog your steps and hold you in an eerie grip: fear, anxiety, shame, lust, addiction, abuse, unemployment. Recalling the power of these things, imagine that the tables are now turned and you've totally triumphed over them. Though once they controlled you, now you control them.

How does it feel? Relish this feeling and remember it. This is what you'll need in order to live a life of joy.

ROUTING THE ENEMY

So the sun stood still, and the moon stopped,

till the nation avenged itself on its enemies.

JOSHUA 10:13

A commitment to joy is a commitment to destroy every enemy of joy. It's not enough to wipe out all our enemies but one. One enemy left standing, unchallenged, casts a shadow over all our joy.

The story of the sun standing still for Joshua is well known, but do we understand why this miracle happened? The reason God stopped the sun in its tracks for a full day was to provide the Israelites with more hours of daylight for chasing and destroying all their enemies.

It takes a long time to mow down five large armies. Killing is hot and heavy work. After the Lord accomplished the lion's share with large hailstones, it would have been easy for the Israelites to call it a day and let the rest of their foes escape—only to have to fight them again another day. So Joshua commanded his troops: "Don't stop! Pursue your enemies, attack them from the rear and don't let them reach their cities, for the LORD your God has given them into your hand" (Joshua 10:19). As a result of Joshua's persistence, he "subdued the whole region.... He left no survivors. He totally destroyed all who breathed, just as the LORD, the God of Israel, had commanded" (Joshua 10:40).

If we find it difficult to comprehend such bloodthirstiness, perhaps we've struck a compromise with our own enemies. Failing to see the metaphor in these Old Testament stories, we reason that our enemies aren't as bad as all that, and it's better to let sleeping dogs lie. We may not even admit we have enemies, because that would mean having to fight them. It seems easier to live with a false peace, never confronting the evil that stalks us. Yet if we want to achieve joy, we must take up the sword.

A friend who had a long struggle with physical illness and depression found great comfort in reading the psalms. However, he commented that he couldn't understand all the brutal passages about enemies, as he felt he had no enemies.

"What about sickness?" I offered. "Or depression? Or shame?"

"Oh," he replied slowly, the light dawning.

By contrast, some Christians like to boast of all the ways they're being attacked by the enemy. To be attacked is considered a badge of spiritual honor, something to be expected in the course of building the kingdom. The ancient Israelites, however, were attacked only when they went astray; their own sin left them vulnerable. Whenever they ardently followed the Lord, however, they became the aggressors, and no enemy could withstand them.

Often in the course of my experiment I had to resolve to go on the offensive and mount a blistering counterattack. I had to stop playing the victim and learn to be the aggressor. I never used to think this way. The idea of attacking my spiritual enemies would have chilled me to the bone. Yet gradually I learned a surprising truth: What matters isn't the force or skill of my attack, but the simple resolution to fight. As long as I hang back in fear, I cannot win. But the moment I take up arms with a will, the enemy's on the run. It's exactly as Scripture says: "Resist the devil, and he will flee from you" (James 4:7).

Once your enemies turn tail, don't just say "good riddance" and let them go. Give chase! Lower your guard in happy times, and the enemy will return more fiercely. The sunshine of joy, far from being an excuse for complacency, is energy for routing the foe.

JOB DESCRIPTION: JOY

So Joshua said to the Israelites: "How long will you wait
before you begin to take possession of the land
that the LORD, the God of your fathers, has given you?"

JOSHUA 18:3

Joy is God's gift, but we must also determinedly take possession of it.
These two sides of the joy equation are equal in importance. We must
not assume that joy can be ours for the taking, for it always comes as a gift.
However, the Lord can give all He likes, but if we won't take it, the gift won't
be ours.

Will you receive the gift of happiness that God offers to all His children?
Will you take possession of it? If I buy a house, I take possession of it and
move in. I don't move in partway; I move in all the way. I possess it completely. This is where the Israelites went wrong. They moved into the
Promised Land, but they didn't move in all the way. They never took possession of it completely. Instead they compromised with their enemies, and so
they compromised their own happiness.

Several reasons lie behind this reluctance to possess the Promised Land.
For one thing, the Israelites were descended from a race of slaves who had
never owned land. Also, this generation was nomadic by nature, not used to
settling down or having anything of their own. It was hard for them to grasp
the vision of possessing an entire country outright. Besides, they were reluctant to challenge the remaining Canaanites for fear of renewing war. Far from
being a warlike people, they were content to leave well enough alone.

Aren't we just like the Israelites when it comes to possessing joy? Joy takes
work, and while we may not mind working hard for material goals, spiritually

we tend to be lazy. Happiness, however, is the proper work of the Christian. Throughout my experiment, whenever people asked me how I was, I could often truthfully answer, "Top of the world! After all, being happy is my job these days." How wonderful to know that my legitimate work in this world, my labor and toil under the sun, was to be joyful!

Since joy requires work, why not take it on as a business or career? What if we gave the pursuit of joy (along with other facets of Christian character) the same energy and devotion we bring to our jobs? If we wake up in the morning and don't feel like going to work, still we go. If we want a paycheck, sloughing off isn't an option. But since nobody pays us to be happy, regularly we call in sick.

Wouldn't it be more fun just to show up at the Happy Factory every morning and do the work, whether we want to or not? Isn't it worth some effort, knowing we'll be paid in the form of an increasingly rich and blissful life?

God's will is done happily or not at all. While we may perform many good works, if we do them without joy, what good are they? A cheerful spirit is the flavoring in our soup; without it the Christian life is bland and unappealing. "You are the salt of the earth. But if the salt loses its saltiness…it is no longer good for anything" (Matthew 5:13). A depressed, grumbling spirit caused an entire generation of Israelites to lose God's favor and die in the desert.

We must get over our feeling that joy is impractical, unachievable, or unworthy of our best efforts. People who are chasing money do not view their goal this way. Why should we, who pursue a goal immeasurably more precious?

THE CHAMPION SPIRIT

In the heavens he has pitched a tent for the sun,

which is like a bridegroom coming forth from his pavilion,

like a champion rejoicing to run his course.

PSALM 19:4-5

The psalmist David knew about champions. He launched his career by defeating "a champion named Goliath" (1 Samuel 17:4), and in David's army special honor was given to champions known as "mighty men." One of David's mighty men "went down into a pit on a snowy day and killed a lion." Another "raised his spear against eight hundred men, whom he killed in one encounter." A champion named Eleazar, when all the rest of the Israelite army retreated, "stood his ground and struck down the Philistines till his hand grew tired and froze to the sword" (2 Samuel 23:20,8-10).

This is the spirit that's needed to win through to a life of joy. Instead of feet that flee from difficulties, we need hands that freeze to our swords. Even *champion* is too weak a word for the true Christian, that roving, dangerous, hoodlum warrior of God. To paraphrase Romans 8:37, "We are more than champions through him who loved us."

Joy lives dangerously. If an experience is deeply satisfying, it usually holds an element of uncertainty. If satisfaction is to enlarge into joy, the uncertainty factor will be high. Risk, peril, unpredictability are the air that joy breathes. Remove these factors and joy suffocates. This is why God has designed for us a life that can be lived only by faith.

Champions sleep in their armor, weapons always at hand. Through constant practice they become invincible, and knowing this makes them jubilant, so much so that they thirst for more and more conquests as they "go from strength to strength" (Psalm 84:7).

Champions don't mind being uncomfortable. If we were on an interstellar voyage, we would accept the inconveniences of space travel as part of the bargain. Why not do the same with life? Even more than *Star Trek*, life offers incomparable opportunities for adventure, discovery, and spectacular beauty. If we're busy complaining about the confinement of our space suit, we might miss it all.

Champions are not afraid of death. At least, they're less afraid of death than they are of not living fully, and so they're prepared to face anything. Revelation 12:11 tells of the saints who "did not love their lives so much as to shrink from death." The moment we take this stance, the devil can do nothing more to us. We're not yet dead, but we've died to everything including death itself. Once dead, we're hidden with Christ and beyond the reach of the enemy. As long as we keep squirming, however, shrinking from hardships and pining for an easier life, the devil still has our number.

The course of a champion requires continual growth. For the person who's growing, each day is different. Each hour presents new challenges that have to be met with new strategies. If we're stuck in a rut, we don't need new strategies; we can live by the same old rules and never change a thing. To joy this is intolerable. Joy requires freshness, newness, stimulation. Joy thrives on the unboxable largeness of life in all its bewildering variety. Depression feeds on sameness, but joy craves a steady diet of fresh, dangerous, wiggling, live game.

Don't just be a survivor of life; be "a champion rejoicing to run his course." Imagine yourself "a bridegroom coming forth from his pavilion," greeting each new day as if it's your wedding day or your last day on earth— or both.

THE NEW CREATION

Be glad and rejoice forever in what I will create,
for I will create Jerusalem to be a delight
and its people a joy.

ISAIAH 65:18

Reading Old Testament passages like the one above, we may presume they apply to a distant future when God will "create new heavens and a new earth" (Isaiah 65:17). The message of the New Testament, however, is that this new creation has already begun. It begins with you and me when we place our faith in Jesus, for "if anyone is in Christ, he is a new creation; the old has gone, the new has come!" (2 Corinthians 5:17). This new creation called a Christian is not just a religious adherent but a brand-new kind of human being, of a species never before seen on earth, belonging to "a holy nation" set apart from all other people and imbued with "the powers of the coming age" (1 Peter 2:9; Hebrews 6:5).

As we new creatures look around us, it may seem that little on earth has changed since Christ initiated His kingdom. The trees seem unaffected, animals are the same, the sky is still in place, the world is more modern but essentially unchanged, and our fellow humans are the same scalawags they've always been. What then has changed?

We have! We're born again, and we have the makings of a new mind, new heart, new will, new feelings, and we even have the rudiments of a new spiritual body with a full set of spiritual senses. We can hear God, and we see, taste, touch, and smell spiritual realities in a way that unbelievers cannot imagine.

This is why Jesus introduced the Eucharist with the words, "Take and eat; this is my body" (Matthew 26:26). Jesus offers His body and blood, His very life, to replace the old creation, our former self. The bread and wine are physical tokens of just how real and tangible is the transformation of our old self into a new creature. In this foretaste of the great heavenly banquet to come, it's as if our proud Father God is slapping His newborn child on the bum and saying, "Breathe! Feel! Eat and drink! You're alive and well in the kingdom of heaven!"

Such thoughts fill me with joy, so much that I can hardly keep up with my fingers as I write. Yes, I know the battle isn't all over yet. I'll continue to struggle with sin for the rest of my earthly life, and yet sin does not express who I really am. "If I do what I do not want to do, *it is no longer I who do it,* but it is sin living in me that does it" (Romans 7:20). Who is this "I" who does not sin? It's the child of God, the new creature, holy, pure, inviolate, utterly beyond the reach of Satan. Already this "I" has crossed over into the Promised Land and is enjoying its blessings, the first of which is joy itself.

The root of joy is the astounding realization that I'm in the kingdom of God *right now.* In this world that kingdom is not yet fully realized, but in me its essentials are already present. Already I've crossed over into the land flowing with milk and honey, where I'm blessed "in the heavenly realms with every spiritual blessing in Christ" (Ephesians 1:3). If the Holy Spirit is like a vine growing inside me, joy hangs in clusters from its branches. Joy is not of this world; it arises from within, from a place so deep within that it's Beyond. By faith I live in that Beyond today. All that's necessary to embrace the overflowing joy of having arrived at this wonderful new life is to "take and eat."

CELEBRATING
COMMUNION

When your words came, I ate them;
they were my joy and my heart's delight.

JEREMIAH 15:16

Again and again in the course of my experiment I found that the greatest joy came from a return to the simple gospel—the gospel of sin forgiven and of release from condemnation. Joylessness might almost be defined as the absence of the experience of personal righteousness. Can you be happy knowing you aren't right with God? However, knowing you've been washed white as snow and are holy, clean clear through, that you share the very righteousness of God and "participate in the divine nature" (2 Peter 1:4)—how could this not produce great joy?

The miracle of the gospel is that a fallen human being can remain a sinner, yet be separated from sin and made wholly righteous, all in one step. We may take many steps, often years, before embracing this mystery thoroughly enough to enjoy a settled sense of our righteousness in Christ. However, the many steps and the many years are not necessary. The miracle all happened in one stupendous step when we first believed in the Lord Jesus.

This one step need never be repeated. As a child my wife gave her life to Christ over and over, never quite believing that the thing had been properly done. Eventually she realized that all this repetition had more to do with paganism than with Christianity. In the Lord's eyes her first commitment stood good for all eternity.

Radios these days can be tuned to a desired frequency with one push of a button. Righteousness, similarly, isn't something we must keep establishing; rather, we're tuned already, and if our station wobbles we can easily adjust it. "If we confess our sins, he is faithful and just and will forgive us our sins and purify us from all unrighteousness" (1 John 1:9). This need not be a long and involved process; it can happen with one push of a button, one short prayer.

I've been at communion services where a great deal was made of self-examination. But the Lord's Supper is not a time to delve into ourselves but to remember Him (Luke 22:19). When Paul warned that "a man ought to examine himself before he eats of the bread and drinks of the cup," it was because the Corinthians were eating and drinking "without recognizing the body of the Lord" (1 Corinthians 11:28-29). The Lord's Supper is a "love feast" (Jude 12) memorializing Christ's death for us and our mystical union with Him and one another. The communion service should emphasize our union with Christ, not our disunion.

The author of Hebrews goes to great lengths to contrast the old Jewish sacrificial system with the new sacrifice of Jesus Christ offered "once for all" (10:10). The old system "can never, by the same sacrifices repeated endlessly year after year, make perfect those who draw near to worship" (10:1). Thanks to Christ, however, "by one sacrifice he has made perfect forever those who are being made holy" (10:14). While the old system could never be more than a regular "reminder of sins" (10:3), in Christ "there is no longer any sacrifice for sin" (10:18).

Is the Eucharist, or the Christian life in general, an endlessly repeated sacrifice that never actually frees us from guilt? How liberating to know that the heart of Christianity is not a dreary rehearsal of our obstinate sinfulness, but a joyous celebration of our union with God through Christ Jesus!

SONG OF HEAVEN

Where were you when I laid the earth's foundation…
while the morning stars sang together
and all the angels shouted for joy?

JOB 38:4,7

Scientists like to talk about the Big Bang, but little do they realize that the echoes they detect may be the shouts of angels. Curled within everything in the universe, no matter how small or big, chaotic or unlikely, lies a seed of joy that was planted there from the beginning. This is what all of reality rests upon. So obvious was this secret at the foundation of all things that it caused the angels to erupt in jubilant celebration. How long will you wait to join them?

Ten years ago I was engaged in writing a long book called *The Gospel According to Job.* I was struggling with depression, and the book was an attempt to come to terms with my own pain and sadness. Though I've traveled a long journey to arrive at the country of joy, it strikes me as ironic that between *Job* and *joy* there's a difference of only one letter.

Sometime when you're feeling low, try reading through the last five chapters of the book of Job. At the end of Job's trials, the Lord comes to him, lifts Job's eyes to the stars and to all the other wonders of creation, and says in effect: While you've been depressed, life has gone on in all its beauty and wonder. The sun keeps rising, the waves of the sea continue to roar, the hawks still fly, the deer and mountain goats give birth. Despite your struggles, flowers bloom, rivers flow, birds sing with piercing sweetness, even "the wings of the ostrich flap joyfully" (39:13). How can you stay gloomy when all of creation bursts with glory? Your sufferings have been real, but far more real is the deep message of life and joy that surrounds you.

At a time when Abram was struggling with doubt and discouragement, the Lord "took him outside and said, 'Look up at the heavens and count the stars—if indeed you can count them.' Then he said to him, 'So shall your offspring be'" (Genesis 15:5). In this scene I don't picture Abram standing and craning his neck; rather I see him lying on a grassy hillside, lost in wonder as the Lord opens his eyes to the splendor of the heavens and the personal message they hold for him. The stars, besides being beautiful in themselves, are pointers to the everlasting joys of heaven. To Abram, to Job, and to us God says: Do you imagine your own heavenly crown to be any less resplendent than the diamond-studded diadem of the night sky?

God knew very well that Abram could never count the stars. If you started now to count stars at the rate of one thousand per second, to count them all would take more than fourteen billion years. Indeed "the heavens declare the glory of God" (Psalm 19:1). By lifting Abram's gaze to the stars, God desired, as with Job, to lift him out of gloom with a glimpse of the birthday candles on his cake.

Are you looking for joy? Look up at the stars. They're remnants of the original creation as it sprang fresh from the furnace of God's thoughts. And they contain, encoded in ancient but luminous script, the great secret at the heart of the cosmos: JOY!

THE MYSTICAL FRIEND

Surely you have granted him eternal blessings
and made him glad with the joy of your presence.

PSALM 21:6

J oy is a presence. When I'm happy it's because I do not feel alone. Gone
is that gnawing core of anxious ache that makes me think I must face
the world alone and handle all my problems without help. Joy fills up this
emptiness with a presence. Indeed this mysterious sense of presence is joy's
chief characteristic. There's a fellowship, a secret companionship, an invisible
embrace. Happiness comes wrapped in warmth because it's literally like being
hugged.

Joy, like love, banishes loneliness. Whereas love is specifically directed
toward another person, joy has a softer focus. If love is the sun, joy is the
moon and the planets—a reflected light. Just as the moon shines only because
of the sun, so we are happy only because of the loving presence of the Other.
We may not be consciously aware of the Other, nevertheless His presence is
the reason for our joy.

To describe joy as a presence is really to call it a Person. This Other Person, this mystical Friend, is Jesus. Even in unbelievers, true happiness is
always a token, a calling card, of Christ. As I write about joy, I'm really writing about Jesus—about what it's like to be with Him, about my longing to be
with Him always, and about my growing certainty that He is always with me.

When I'm not joyful, it's because I don't feel myself in the Lord's presence. To quote an old chorus, "Joy is the flag flown high from the castle of my
heart when the King is in residence there." Whenever I hear and receive His

Word in my heart, the result is always joy, because the voice of the Lord is the voice of joy, His face is alive with joy, and His eyes are shining, merry eyes.

Joy is a Person. To know this is to know the Holy Spirit as not an *It* but a *Who*. Knowing Him is like having a dear husband or wife or a much loved brother or sister: We know these people will not desert us, so we don't have to keep them under our thumb. Without worry we can let them come and go, safe in the knowledge that even when they're not bodily present with us, still our relationship is secure.

My wife once gave me an anniversary card that read, on the outside, "I have everything I need to be happy." The inside said, "I have you." Happiness isn't in ourselves but in others and our Lord. Paul wrote to the Thessalonians, "What is our hope, our joy, or the crown in which we will glory in the presence of our Lord Jesus when he comes? Is it not you? Indeed, you are our glory and joy" (1 Thessalonians 2:19-20).

God is love; He is also joy. The fact that joy is a Person, rather than something I produce from within myself, is exactly what is so wonderful about it. When I'm on personal terms with joy, knowing Him as the One who deeply loves me and is committed to me forever, then I shed my suspicions about happiness disappearing and leaving me desolate. The personalness of joy is precisely why happiness is not (contrary to popular belief) fickle by nature, but the opposite—faithful and constant. Feelings come and go, but the presence of God in Jesus can be known, fondly recalled, and embraced at every moment of every day, forever, without limit. He has given His word, "Surely I am with you always" (Matthew 28:20), and joy accompanies Him.

No Condemnation

Why are you downcast, O my soul?
Why so disturbed within me?
Put your hope in God.

PSALM 42:5

One mistake I made throughout my experiment was to think it was somehow up to me to make joy happen. If I wasn't as joyful today as I had been yesterday, I'd worry, "What am I doing wrong?" Or worse, "What's wrong with me?"

This isn't the way of joy at all. The moment I start wondering if something's wrong with me, an anxiety sets in that bars me from joy. As long as I'm anxious, I cannot be joyful. The path to joy is through trust in my Lord, not distrust of myself.

True, I will never trust God if I don't have a basic distrust of myself. But distrust of self is faith's prerequisite, not its continuing focus. Faith holds fast to Jesus. Joy comes not through abasing myself but through exalting Jesus.

The question *What's wrong with me?* was answered the day I became a Christian. What's wrong is that I'm a sinner and always will be in this life. So what else is new?

What's new is that Jesus takes away my sin and removes it "as far as the east is from the west" (Psalm 103:12), and "there is now no condemnation for those who are in Christ Jesus" (Romans 8:1). The good news of redemption, not the stale news of sin, is the Christian's obsession.

I cannot be joyful if I continue to harbor a nagging feeling that, in spite of all Jesus has done, there remains something wrong with me. More than just doubting myself, this is doubting God. The Lord may be ever so wonderful, but if I think He has failed with me, I secretly view Him as a failure. Unhappiness is ungodliness.

Many of us could benefit from taking ten minutes a day not just to count our blessings, but to count the ways we bless others. Instead of dwelling on the bad in ourselves, what if we deliberately took time to dwell on our good qualities? So much unhappiness derives from poor self-image. How can we be happy if we don't see ourselves as gifted, righteous, pure, beautiful? How can we be happy about a holy God if we persist in seeing ourselves as unholy? Rather than running ourselves down, we need to agree with God who has "raised us up with Christ and seated us with him in the heavenly realms" (Ephesians 2:6). To believe in God is to believe also in ourselves.

Do you believe the gospel? Do you believe Jesus has literally taken away all your sin? It's one thing to glimpse this truth in moments of insight, but has it sunk in that you can actually live this way—every day, all day long, without *any* condemnation? Can you bear this? Can you stand to know the truth about yourself, however glorious it may be? Or are you too used to dragging around that load of guilt and shame, trying to pay for your own sins and worrying your way to heaven?

In Bunyan's classic *Pilgrim's Progress,* when Christian finally arrives at the cross and the open tomb, the great burden he's been carrying "fell from off his back, and began to tumble, and so continued to do, till it came to the mouth of the Sepulchre, where it fell in, and I saw it no more." Then Christian "gave three leaps for joy."[7]

The realization of the gospel is always accompanied by a total release from condemnation and a resulting lighthearted joy. This is how we know we're in touch with the real thing and have not been led astray.

DIVINE CONSPIRACY

He was filled with joy because he had come to believe in God.

ACTS 16:34

D oes your faith in God fill you with joy? Is God alone reason enough to rejoice, or are you looking for something more? If you're not satisfied with God, what more could you possibly want?

Paul told the Philippian jailer, "Believe in the Lord Jesus, and you will be saved" (Acts 16:31). Not only was the man saved, he was filled with joy, because the two go together. Do they for you? If you've got God, you've got joy. If you don't have joy, however religious you may be, you need to wonder whether you've really got hold of God. Joy, besides being desirable in itself, is a litmus test of the truth.

That church you attend—is it full of joy? If not, it's missing the mark of truth.

The preaching you listen to—does it inspire you with joy? If not, it falls short of the gospel.

Your friendships—do they produce joy? If not, what good are they?

Those activities you pursue so doggedly—do you take joy in them? If not, why bother?

The book you're reading—does it stir joy deep inside? If not, why read it?

Joy is a trustworthy guide to the truth. Where joy is absent, we're right to be suspicious, because joy is a characteristic of truth. It is not truth's only trait; there are other marks to look for. But any teaching that doesn't bear the mark of joy falls short of the whole truth. At times other aspects of truth (such as holiness or justice) may predominate, but where these other characteristics exist without a strong undercurrent of telltale joy—watch out!

While joy itself is not the truth, it illuminates or identifies truth. It's the light shining on the signpost at night, telling us we're on the right road. Joy is like the smile on the face of a loving friend. If we're in a strange city and meet a familiar face in the crowd, yet receive no smile of greeting or recognition, we know something's wrong. It's a case of mistaken identity.

Why are we so quick to mistake our good friend joy and take up with some stranger? Does the rigorous litmus test of joy seem too demanding? What would happen if we gave joy its rightful authority? If we trusted joy enough to let it lead us, how much grief, how many wrong turns, how much needless perplexity might we avoid?

My friend Burt Rosenberg has a "ministry of joy." He travels around to churches telling jokes, clowning, poking fun at pastors and elders, getting people laughing and having a good time. Then, when everyone's too drunk on joy to notice, he slips deep truth in among the hilarity. Burt believes "the kingdom of God is a divine conspiracy to smuggle joy into the world." Describing himself as a "co-conspirator," his goal is "to help straighten out the decline of civilization through the release of joy inside of people."[8]

The world, despite all its apparent offers of pleasure, is organized against joy, with a campaign as militant as it is subtle. There are so many ways to live joylessly. One needn't be obviously depressed; one may feel merely wistful, vaguely bored, a bit dull, somewhat trapped. One may lead a productive life and have a lot of good times. But where is joy?

Of all the world's teachings, only the true gospel of Jesus Christ contains the joy to penetrate this deadly facade. Jesus alone offers real, enduring joy. This, in fact, is how we know Him.

SONG AND DANCE

After David had killed the Philistine, the women came out
from all the towns of Israel to meet King Saul with singing
and dancing, with joyful songs and with tambourines and lutes.

1 SAMUEL 18:6

When I told a friend I was writing a book on joy, immediately she asked, "Is there anything in it about dancing?" Her flashing black eyes seemed to add, "If not, it won't be worth reading."

She's right. If the words of this book don't get off the page and dance around, and inspire readers to do the same, I've failed. Joy isn't about words but about a flow of energy that changes lives. Similarly dancing isn't a physical activity only, but a spiritual one. A good dance changes something in the dancer, in the world around, in the very atmosphere.

On a summer holiday with my family, it rained for a solid week. I like rain—it's great reading weather—but my daughter was climbing the walls. During a family worship time, one song got us up on our feet and dancing. You've heard of rain dances? Suddenly I said, "Why not do a sun dance to our God?" So we danced with joyful abandon, and the next day the sun came out and we had fair weather the rest of our holiday.

Some prayers must be danced, and some prayers must be sung. Without the singing and the dancing, they won't rise to heaven. Song and dance must be done with all the heart—or why bother?—and this in itself effects a change. The very act of throwing oneself utterly into an activity releases joy. So often we hang back from life, but spend a night dancing your heart out and see how it feels. Then approach work, marriage, church, everything this way. A life of joy requires giving oneself a hundred percent.

Music, a gift we share with the angels, has the power to bypass rational thought and plunge us into unselfconscious innocence. When people open their mouths and sing, they even look different, pure and natural. This happens still more with dancing. Often when I pray for people, or if I'm just seeking to understand them better, I'll imagine them dancing. Here's a teenage girl so caught up in how she looks, so high-strung and insecure, and I picture her perfectly relaxed and waltzing in the arms of Jesus. Or here's a conservative, buttoned-up old gentleman who has never truly celebrated for five minutes in his life, and I see him throwing out his arms, tossing back his head, and kicking up his heels in a rapturous jig. I try to see people as they would be if their customary reserve were suddenly uncorked and the champagne of their souls came bubbling out. In ecstatic release their true self emerges, and seeing this, I know how to pray for them with love. That stiff old fogy—who would have guessed he had so much zest in him? But he does! This is who he is, if only he knew it. As Yeats wrote,

An aged man is but a paltry thing,
A tattered coat upon a stick, unless
Soul clap its hands and sing, and louder sing
For every tatter in its mortal dress.[9]

A dance, like a face or a fingerprint, is a mark of identity. Even in my imagination each individual does a dance no one else on earth could do. It's hard to treat people as being free and harder still for them to see themselves that way. But it's not so difficult to picture them cutting loose and tripping the light fantastic. Surely this is how God likes to see us, as singers and dancers around His throne. He sees us happy and free, as He made us. He's always coaxing us to let down our hair and come to His party.

STRETCH EVERY DAY

With your help I can advance against a troop;
with my God I can scale a wall.

PSALM 18:29

I was a full-time writer for nearly twenty years before I ever did a radio interview. I had plenty of opportunities, but I always said no. I told myself I was a writer, not a public speaker. This was one reason, and a legitimate one. The other reason was fear.

I did my first radio interview during my experiment in joy. I had to, because I'd promised myself to do a stretch every day. A stretch is something difficult that I sense will be good for me. It moves me out of my comfort zone so I can grow. I do a stretch not because it's easy or fun, but because I want the growth that comes from having done it. Sometimes the difficulty of a stretch vanishes the moment I step into it; other times the exhilaration of victory is delayed. One thing's for sure: A stretch holds no benefit at all if I never do it. To reap rewards I must push the plow.

The day I did my first radio interview, if you'd been with me in the room you would have seen me literally shaking like a leaf. When it was all over, however, I got a big surprise: I wasn't prepared for how gloriously happy I felt. To quote a favorite line from a novel, my "smile was so wide you would have had to break it into sections to fit it through a door."[10]

Why? Because I'd burst through a wall. I faced a crippling fear head-on, and by God's grace I overcame it. For the next interview I was still fearful, but I didn't shake. By the third interview, though I was nervous, the fear was gone, and after that it was smooth sailing. I doubt I could have written this book if I hadn't accepted the challenge to do interviews. Overcoming one significant fear has a ripple effect throughout an entire life.

Two years later, incidentally, I decided to quit doing interviews. This time, however, I knew it was for good reasons and not out of fear. Saying yes had been a stretch, and now saying no was also a stretch. Both decisions emerged from my resolve to follow joy wherever she might lead.

Living in joy requires doing a stretch every day. Tackle that unpleasant task you've been putting off; make that phone call; go for that job interview; initiate that delicate conversation. You know what needs doing. Life will stretch you anyway; why not take it by surprise and do your own stretching deliberately? If you don't choose your stretches, they'll be assigned to you. God wants you to know the joy of continuous growth and victory. "A ship in a harbor is safe," goes a saying, "but that's not what ships were built for."

I like novelist E. L. Konigsburg's definition of happiness as "excitement that has found a settling down place, but there is always a little corner that keeps flapping around."[11] Often people are unhappy because they resist change, always buttoning down what should be flapping around. If they were guaranteed happiness as a reward, they might be willing to make one or two small changes, but instinctively they know it wouldn't stop there. Remaining happy would require more and more changes, until continuous growth became a lifestyle. By digging in their heels and making changes only under duress, they never know the joy of abandoning themselves to a God whose purposes for His children are so unlimited that there's no time for coasting.

CATCH THE WAVE

Let the rivers clap their hands,
let the mountains sing together for joy.

PSALM 98:8

I love the sound of the word *joy*. To my ears it's onomatopoeic—a word that sounds like what it means. Say *joy* out loud a few times and see if it doesn't bring a lift to your spirit.

One day I was walking by the ocean when I heard the word *joy* being spoken by the waves. As each breaker curled over and undid itself like a foaming zipper along the beach, it was as if the crashing walls of water were uttering over and over the sound "J-J-J-J-J-J-J-J-J-O-Y!" Is this what the psalmist heard when he described rivers clapping their hands?

I enjoy body-surfing, which is done with a short board that you hug to your body. As with normal surfing, you paddle out into the waves, hang around until a big one comes, then ride its crest into shore. Typically you'll make several attempts before getting a good ride. A big wave may take you nowhere if your timing is off, but if you catch even a medium wave just right, something almost supernatural happens. You feel power surge beneath you like an engine, and you can be carried an incredible distance. Talk about a joy ride! Each time that mysterious engine kicks in and lifts me like a dolphin on its back, I laugh and shout out loud.

Surfing isn't much fun if you don't know how to catch the wave. The same is true of joy. There's no shortage of joy—it's like waves rolling in, one after another—but you have to catch them. This book was a catch-the-wave phenomenon. When the idea of doing an experiment in joy first came to me, I wanted to put it off until I was "ready." I know now that if I'd postponed my experiment I never would have done it. Just as Jesus performed miracles when "the power of the Lord was present" (Luke 5:17), for me the Lord's power was present for entering into joy. I had to catch the wave.

One morning during my experiment, I woke up feeling foggy and sluggish, tired of thinking about joy and wishing I could take a break from it. Despairingly I recalled that I was scheduled to be interviewed on a national radio program at eleven o'clock that morning. At eight, however, the phone rang, a voice asked if I was ready, and three minutes later I was on the air live, addressing a million listeners. What a way to wake up! Not long into the interview I found myself talking enthusiastically, for the first time in public, about my experiment in joy. By the end of the broadcast I felt as bubbly as if I'd just had a bath in pink champagne.

How did joy come to me that day? Just as it always comes—as a complete surprise. By its very nature joy is full of surprises. Isn't the unknown an essential ingredient of a happy experience? The surprise factor brings me news that the God who is far bigger than I am is alive and well and up to His marvels.

At the heart of this book lies a paradox: While I can deliberately plan and choose to be joyful, I can never plan exactly how joy will happen. Each day it surprises me, because surprise is a part of joy's nature. Each day I have to bob around in the waves, waiting for the big one, and when I catch it I shout and gasp with pleasure. And then I paddle out again, knowing there's always another wave of joy where the last one came from.

THE ULTIMATE SACRIFICE

At his tabernacle will I sacrifice with shouts of joy;
I will sing and make music to the LORD.

PSALM 27:6

J oy is free but it's not cheap. Joy comes dear; it involves a sacrifice. If I'm not joyful, something is standing between me and joy. What is it? Am I willing to give that thing up? Will I surrender my anger? Will I let go of pride and ambition? Will I give up thinking that my circumstances need to change before I can be joyful? What's so important that I allow it to over-shadow joy?

Read Psalm 27 and you'll find it full of "war," "trouble," "violence," and "enemies." Yet all this didn't stop David from sacrificing "with shouts of joy." The psalmist knew how to shake free of trouble with a psalm. That's what the psalms are—sacrifices of joy. David knew God's pleasure is not in dead animals or rituals but in what happens in the human heart. If the heart doesn't engage joyfully in worship, or at least emerge from worship rejoicing, then the sacrifice is incomplete. The ultimate sacrifice we can offer the Lord is the sacrifice of joy.

Many of the psalms begin in joy, and those that don't start on a high note usually end that way. As the psalmist enters the presence of God, no matter how burdened he may be, there's a movement from negative to positive. The heart lifts as all that weighs it down is sacrificed. If I want to be happy in Jesus, I must begin by setting aside all other goals. I make it my one ambition to bless the Lord in all circumstances, to love Him no matter what, to worship Him always, to remain in Him, to be constantly and eternally grateful. As I do this, the secrets of joy open up.

For the person committed to joy, so many roads are no longer open—scorn, impatience, complaining, criticism. When all such easy and habitual options are cut off, a wonderful clarification takes place in the spirit. The dross settles out, leaving room only for the gold of joy.

Joy is the ultimate sacrifice. Sometimes in a mood of reckless thankfulness I'll pray, "Lord, You've done so much for me. What can I do for You in return?" Seldom have I received a specific answer to this prayer, for simply by praying it I'm already offering the Lord the greatest gift possible—a joyful heart. Being joyful in Him means I've already given Him everything else; I hold nothing back.

Once when I gave blood at a Red Cross clinic, a small red sticker was placed on my lapel. Shaped like a drop of blood, it bore these words: *Be nice to me. I gave blood today.* When I arrived home, in a moment of inspiration I stuck this sticker on my crucifix. And there it stayed for a long time, reminding me that Jesus gave His blood for me and that I owe Him my very life. Every day He continues to give and give, sustaining my life in every way. The least I can do in return is to be nice to Him by being happy about what He's done.

For years I went around expecting God to be nice to me and wondering why He wasn't. I had to learn this rule: Be nice to Jesus and He'll be nice to you. He's nice to you anyway, but without joy you won't notice it. Why not thank and praise the Lord, giving Him the sacrifice of joy by being a happy Christian?

Good Medicine

A cheerful heart is good medicine,
but a crushed spirit dries up the bones.

Proverbs 17:22

During my experiment I was curious about the relationship between joy and physical health. I wondered if the disciplined practice of joy might protect me from illness. It didn't. During much of the second month I struggled with sickness, and this forced me to study the topic more carefully.

I met with some surprising results. For example, some of my most joyful times in all the ninety days came when I felt the most ill. Joy feels different in a body weakened by disease. It's lovelier than ever, with a light, graceful ethereality so obviously supernatural, so clearly at odds with what a person in pain ought to experience.

One evening during family prayers I felt so sick that I asked the others to pray for me. I had no strength or will to pray myself; nevertheless when my turn came, I opened my mouth and was surprised to hear words coming out. Before I knew it, I was offering the most beautiful, tender, exquisitely worded prayer as tears streamed down my face. Where did this come from? It came straight from God in heaven, the same way joy kept coming and coming throughout my experiment.

Truly my marriage with the Lord is "for better, for worse; in sickness and in health." So much joy came to me in sickness that I kept taking it as a sign that I would be miraculously healed. I wasn't. Several times I experienced dramatic joy only to find myself sicker a few hours later. In the end I got better gradually, and all my attempts to discern some spiritual pattern in my healing came to nothing. Happiness, I concluded, while it's definitely good medicine, is not necessarily a ticket to wellness.

For me the riddle of joy and health remains unsolved as long as there are Christians who are radiantly happy in the Lord, yet who nevertheless bear diseases for which they cannot find healing. As a friend with angina put it, "There's nothing like chronic heart pain to change your theology." The trouble with a triumphalist theology of perfect health (besides the obvious fact that sooner or later everyone dies) is that it segregates believers into classes—the well who have great faith and the sick who have little. Is it possible that I do the same with my theology of joy? The difference, I think, is that if one must choose between health and happiness as goals, by all means choose happiness. Too close a focus on physical health is unhealthy; the focus should rather be on glorifying God in all circumstances. What sustains one in suffering is not the hope of glowing health but the joy of the Lord.

Having said all this, I must add that since becoming a disciple of joy, in general I've been healthier than ever. If "a cheerful heart is good medicine," clearly a relationship exists between joy and wellness. Therefore rejoice! Happiness suits us well. Whatever our condition, when we're happy we function better both physically and spiritually. We're more alert, productive, and helpful to others. Joy looks good on us because we're made for it. Put misery in your tank and see how far you get. Then try a little joy—laugh with friends, play with children, "sing and make music in your heart to the Lord" (Ephesians 5:19)—and feel the vigor of youth flow back into your bones.

COMPASSION

Shout for joy, O heavens; rejoice, O earth;
burst into song, O mountains!
For the LORD comforts his people
and will have compassion on his afflicted ones.

ISAIAH 49:13

I'd like to say that during my experiment I faced some horrendous trials and came through with flying colors. But no, it was all pretty ordinary stuff. The most serious problem I encountered, I'm ashamed to say, was marital conflict. Karen and I have a strong relationship with little fighting. During my three-month experiment in joy, however, we locked horns more frequently and more seriously than we have in the three years since. Here was the one obstacle to my joy that most resisted resolution.

I recall a friend saying that whenever he was attacked, the attack came most often through his family. Is it possible that Karen was drawing fire for me as I made advances in joy? All I know is that as I grew happier, I watched her go the other way, toward increased anxiety, overwork, and a lingering sadness. This was odd, because Karen by nature is more cheerful than I, and the change in her distressed me. Whenever I tried to broach this subject, inviting her to slow down and smell the flowers, her eyes glazed over, and I knew she wasn't hearing me. This was aggravating. Something seemed to be preventing her from moving toward joy.

Something was—a family problem beyond her ability to resolve. For a long time I was blind to the depth of her struggle. When finally the Lord opened my eyes and I saw clearly what was happening, I saw also that all my efforts to communicate joy to Karen were in vain. As much as I wanted her to join me on my journey, she either could not or would not. No, the only answer was for me to join her, to meet her in her sadness. Instead of trying to change her, I needed to pray for her, to love her, to have compassion. Instead of being threatened by her distress, I needed to embrace it as my own. As I did so, joy flowed back into our marriage.

Many times the Lord has warned me not to become so happy that I lose compassion for those in distress. I'm a slow learner, however, and it's easy for someone of my temperament to err on the side of spiritual intensity. Marriage, along with other relationships, is the best corrective for this excess. Hence Peter advises husbands to "be considerate as you live with your wives…so that nothing will hinder your prayers" (1 Peter 3:7).

All spirituality must be normalized and validated in relationships. The joy of the Lord cannot be achieved in isolation; we must involve others, and normally this happens less through words than by example. While our sermons may not be received gladly, compassion opens a channel for joy to be shared.

Love takes precedence over joy. Have compassion for others, for to the extent that one tries to ignore or push away their unhappiness, one's own pursuit of happiness will be frustrated. Joy need not recoil from suffering, because joy is strong enough to carry both its own pain and that of others. A truly happy person understands the reasons others cannot be happy right now, even if those reasons are not condoned. Joy can remain joyful and still feel sorrow for the whole world.

FRUIT OF THE SPIRIT

The fruit of the Spirit is love, joy, peace, patience,
kindness, goodness, faithfulness, gentleness and self-control.
Against such things there is no law.

GALATIANS 5:22-23

Paul's familiar catalog of the fruit of the Spirit has a logical progression. It's no accident joy is listed second, after love and before peace, because joy really is less important than love and more important than peace. I've experienced the kind of "joy" that is without love and I want no more of it. I also know what it is to have peace—real peace—yet without much joy. I don't know how this is possible, but it is.

The reason joy comes second, following love, is that love governs joy. Anyone who lives a life full of love will be joyful. Conversely, without love there can be no true joy. Private, independent joy is an illusion. Joy exists in, never out of, loving relationships. Love is the shepherd, the keeper, the safeguard of joy. Similarly, as love governs joy, so love and joy together govern all the other fruit of the Spirit. If we think we can be patient or good without being loving and joyful, we're only fooling ourselves. No one else will be fooled by our strained efforts at virtue.

Having said this, it's also true that without patience or goodness we'll have no joy. All nine qualities listed in Galatians 5 require some form of sacrifice. If I want patience, I must give up impatience. If I want gentleness, I must give up anger and manipulation. One reason joy comes near the top of the list is that in order to obtain it I must make significant headway in all the other qualities. To have lasting joy I must be consistently patient, faithful, gentle, and so on. If I'm not joyful, it may be because I've done nothing kind or good today. One simple act of kindness can be all it takes to throw open the gates of joy. Last on the list of spiritual fruit comes self-control, without which all the other qualities, including joy, will be unstable.

So where do we start—at the top of the list or at the bottom? The fruit of the Spirit is not a series of virtues to be practiced in order, so much as the end product of a change of heart. Just as fruit forms naturally on a healthy plant, so joy emerges from a good grasp of the message of the gospel. Before a plant can produce, it must receive well the gifts of water, sunshine, and nourishment. While it's true that I may sometimes obtain joy through being kind, it's much better if my kindness is informed by joy in the first place—the joy that springs from knowing God's kindness for myself.

Notice that Paul speaks in this passage not of many "fruits" but of one fruit, a single entity. The fruit of the Spirit is less like a bowl of apples, oranges, and pears than like a blackberry—one compound, organic whole. Joy, like one small bead of the blackberry, does not grow independently from the rest of the fruit. All the beads join together to form one ensemble, and it's in the context of this collectivity that joy exists.

Paul ends his list with the astounding comment, "Against such things there is no law." Many of us live as if there's a law against joy. We feel we can't be happy because of all the work we have to do and the responsibilities we carry. Jesus wants us to be responsible, but not at the expense of joy. "Look at the birds of the air; they do not sow or reap" (Matthew 6:26). The joyful person, unburdened as a bird, lives beyond rules and mere duties, a law unto himself.

LET GOD BE RIGHT

Your statutes are my heritage forever;

they are the joy of my heart.

PSALM 119:111

At the beginning of this book is a quote from Brother Lawrence: "I do not know what God wishes to do with me; I am always very happy."[12] I chose this epigraph for two reasons. First, Brother Lawrence's outrageous claim to be "always very happy" was a challenge and an inspiration to me. If he could achieve this state, perhaps I could too. Secondly, I was struck by the way the two halves of his statement reflect each other. His thought could almost be expressed the other way around: "I am always very happy" *because* "I do not know what God wishes to do with me." For most people, not knowing God's plans is a source of anxiety. For Brother Lawrence, not knowing was a source of joy. He was happy no matter what the Lord might do.

An experiment in joy is a resolution to give up all doubts about God. As Jesus said to Thomas, "Stop doubting and believe" (John 20:27). Negative feelings are rooted in the suspicion, however subtle, that God may be in the wrong, or at least is not truly concerned with our well-being, and therefore cannot be trusted. The only solution to this impasse is to let God be right. More than just giving Him the benefit of the doubt, we must tell Him unreservedly that He's right and congratulate Him for it. We must choose to worship Him flat out, celebrating His righteousness and justice. By doing whatever it takes to elevate God above ourselves, we tap into the wellspring of joy.

Joy instinctively sides with God in everything, against human circumstances, against transient feelings, against common sense. Common sense does not yield joy; joy is supernatural sense. To attain the supernatural I must adopt God's point of view. Therefore I resolve to let God be right about everything. Instead of being sorry for myself, I let God be right for allowing my sickness or my difficulties to continue. Instead of worrying, I let God be right for not immediately intervening.

Joy comes from thinking God's thoughts, doing His will, looking at everything through His eyes by the power of the indwelling Spirit. To embrace entirely God's point of view, however briefly, is to be joyful. This is true even when God's point of view involves sorrow over suffering. Joy is not proud, detached, or affected. It mixes well with suffering; it comprehends and effectively ministers to loss. Even in the midst of compassion for affliction, everyone who sides with God remains joyful.

Of the ninefold fruit of the Spirit in Galatians 5:22, joy is the one that most takes God's side. All the other qualities identify deeply with people in their weakness; indeed human weakness is the very reason we must exercise patience, kindness, gentleness, and the rest. Joy alone sides entirely with God over and against all the dark struggles of this world. Rather than trying to build a bridge between heaven and earth, joy stands with both feet planted firmly in the kingdom of heaven and calls out boldly, "There's no cause for sadness! No matter what the circumstances, be happy in the Lord!"

A blanket acquiescence to the Lord's will—and not only to His will but to His ways—is the high cost of joy. Even if we're convinced that God's ends for us are good, we may still question His means. Joy gives up all this questioning and hands the Lord a blank check, saying, "Write upon it whatever You will; I'll gladly agree." Joy, by definition, does everything gladly.

Shortcut to Happiness

Consider it pure joy, my brothers, whenever you face trials
of many kinds, because you know that the testing
of your faith develops perseverance.

JAMES 1:2-3

Anyone can "consider it pure joy" when everything goes well. The time when such an attitude really counts is when "you face trials of many kinds." Happy people can have just as many problems as unhappy ones. The difference is that unhappy people hate having problems, whereas happy people are content to work through their problems, finding joy in spite of and even because of them. Joy doesn't result from avoiding suffering but from moving through it. If there's a shortcut to happiness, it's through trials.

Note that James speaks of "many kinds" of trials. Our natural tendency is to treat suffering not as one thing but to categorize it into different types and degrees. This way we can always find an excuse for putting our own trials into a special category that renders them immune from joy. Other people, we reason, may find joy in suffering, but their suffering is not of the same kind or intensity as ours. Or perhaps we found joy in last week's trials, but we see our situation this week as entirely different.

James puts a stop to such prevarications by reducing all suffering to one category. Though we face "trials of many kinds," still they have in common that all may be counted as pure joy. As simpleminded as this sounds, a complicated view of life does not produce joy. The soul of joy is simplicity. Scripture wouldn't tell us to consider trials as "pure joy" unless this were actually possible.

Of course in the thick of difficulties we won't always feel as happy as clams. James's word *consider* suggests less a feeling than an act of faith—that is, in troubled times we count on joy being stored up for us as in a bank account. Then, when the trouble passes, we'll feel a flood of joy as all that has been stored up is poured out.

Doesn't this ring true to experience? Joy doesn't come in a steady stream but in waves. When the stream is blocked for a while, the river of joy keeps on flowing, so that when the blockage is removed all that we missed is suddenly restored in a great outpouring. Knowing this, we can begin in faith to draw upon our storehouse of joy even in distress.

Scott Peck's book *The Road Less Traveled* has a memorable opening:

> Life is difficult. This is a great truth, one of the greatest truths. It is a great truth because once we truly see this truth, we transcend it. Once we truly know that life is difficult—once we truly understand and accept it—then life is no longer difficult. Because once it is accepted, the fact that life is difficult no longer matters…. Life is a series of problems. Do we want to moan about them or solve them?[13]

If we think it unreasonable to expect ourselves to rejoice in suffering, try looking at the other side: Isn't it unreasonable *not* to rejoice? Taking into account God's great love and faithfulness, and the promise of our eternal reward in heaven, isn't a joyless attitude like a small child's tantrum? Feeling powerless, we either shut down or throw a fit as the only means of retaliating against the one who does hold power.

Unhappiness is a form of pouting. It's a way of saying, "I shouldn't have to suffer like this; it's scandalous; I don't deserve it and I won't accept it." Fine. Your unhappiness will continue until you do accept it. You'd rather be right than happy.

CHASED BY THE LIGHT

Light is shed upon the righteous
and joy on the upright in heart.

PSALM 97:11

J im Brandenburg, a photographer with years of experience and many awards, reached a point where he found it necessary to return to basics and renew the deep springs of his art. Accustomed to shooting rolls and rolls of film, for a period of ninety days he resolved to take only one photograph a day. The results of this unusual undertaking were published in *National Geographic* and ultimately in a beautiful book entitled *Chased by the Light.* In all ninety of these photographs, one senses the remarkable integrity of this daring experiment.

Brandenburg's book helped to inspire my experiment in joy. Coincidentally, our two experiments covered approximately the same seasonal period, beginning in late fall and progressing through the darkest days of winter. One day in December when my joy was at a low ebb, I was reminded of one photograph in *Chased by the Light,* which to me is the most striking image in the book. It shows a single red maple leaf floating in a dark still pond against a background of reflected tall grasses. Upon first looking at this picture it may seem rather ordinary, yet it has a haunting quality. That one vibrant, translucent leaf—somehow both pale and bright upon the dark water—seems to hold within it the soul of autumn, that season when joy and sadness, beauty and death, share the same face.

The author's account of how he took this photo, the only one allowed him that day, is worth quoting:

It was late and I despaired of capturing anything of value. The day was dark and gloomy; my mood reflected the weather. I wandered through the dripping forest all day long. Tired, hungry, and wet, I was near tears. I was mentally beating myself for having passed up several deer portraits and the chance to photograph a playful otter. None of those scenes spoke to me at the time.

But perhaps because I was patient, and perhaps because, as natives do on a vision quest, I had reached my physical limits, I became open to the possibility revealed by a single red maple leaf floating on a dark-water pond. My spirits rose the instant I saw it, and although the day was very late and what little light there had been was fleeing rapidly, I studied the scene from every angle. Finally, unsure of my choice, I made the shot anyway, thankful at least that the long day had ended.[14]

The instant I read this passage my spirits rose. Like Brandenburg, I felt at the limit of my endurance that day, unsure of how to renew joy. His words reminded me that great revelation may lie hidden in uncertainty, exhaustion, despair.

Often when joy seems to fade, I recall Jim Brandenburg's idea of allowing himself only one photograph per day. Then, turning my mental camera upon the day I'm living, I seek to locate in it the one moment that holds the most joy. No matter how dull or stressful my day may seem, a point of light always gleams. The more I focus on the light, the larger and brighter it becomes. By nourishing one ray of joy like a seedling, joy takes root in me and grows and grows until it fills my heart.

Are you at the end of your light? Right around the next corner a bright red leaf shines for you in a still pool. Even now your world holds an infinite number of such glimpses of mysterious beauty—hidden in a nearby forest, in your home, even in the concrete jungle, or perhaps in a talk with a friend. One of these shining mysteries, today, is just for you. Open your shutter quickly and take it in.

HIDDEN JOY

At that time Jesus, full of joy through the Holy Spirit, said,
"I praise you, Father, Lord of heaven and earth,
because you have hidden these things from the wise and learned,
and revealed them to little children. Yes, Father,
for this was your good pleasure."

LUKE 10:21

Not quite two months into my experiment, on December 21—the shortest, darkest day of the year—the sun came out for the first time following weeks of rain. On a drive in the country I gazed with wonder at the sun-bathed landscape. Though the fields were bare and wintry, the colors of the earth and dry grasses were subtly glorious, shining translucently beneath veils of mist that seemed about to lift on a new creation.

That evening, as I wrote about joy in my journal, I was surprised to discover that seeing the delicate coloring of the sunlit fields was the high point of my day, the thing that gave me the deepest joy. The day held other joys, but the sight of those colors stood far above all else. Seeing them again in my mind, once again I drank deeply of their joy.

The exercise of examining my life to see where joy lies hidden often yields surprises. It seems I do not know myself, or what makes me happy, as well as I might think. As I look back over a day, slight details, all but unnoticed at the time, may rise to the surface. Surveying these unexpected treasures, I ask myself why they come to mind, why they pique joy in me. After identifying the source of pleasure, I immerse myself in the sensation and let it grow within me. In this way I come to know myself better, to understand what is truly life-giving for me.

The process just described circumvents artificial pleasures to uncover real ones. I believe anyone who honestly follows this process will be surprised at how much hidden joy is already present in a life that may seem humdrum, hectic, or even depressed. Since Jesus is a king in exile, the realities of His kingdom are present incognito, making it necessary for God to smuggle them into our lives almost when we aren't looking. If joy came to us too obviously, through the grand and official channels touted by the world, we'd immediately set to work analyzing and bureaucratizing the life out of it.

Yet why are we so slow to appreciate, why do we even studiously ignore, the very things that bring us deep joy? No doubt it's because the moment we awaken to joy we feel (rightly) responsible to give it expression, to allow more opportunities for its release. This can be unsettling to our cherished routines. If driving in the country makes me happy, I may need to do more of it. If I love the colors of nature, why not spend more time looking? Do I esteem joy so little that I won't cross the street to get some?

Sadly, we have our own stubborn ideas of what should make us happy, and these ideas we pursue with astonishing persistence, however poorly they work. A decision to align our lives with what actually makes us happy, rather than with what we think makes us happy, requires courage, discipline, and a docile spirit. It requires listening to the quiet, lovely voice of the Joy Giver in our hearts and falling into harmony with Him.

Joy need not be sought outside of the lives we already have. No, it lies right under our noses, often in the most ordinary experiences. If we spent the next year simply enjoying who we are and what we have, we'd be much further ahead than by striving for more. What we need most, more than something dramatically new, is a quiet realization of what already is.

JUST SITTING

The LORD your God is with you, he is mighty to save.
He will take great delight in you,
he will quiet you with his love,
he will rejoice over you with singing.

ZEPHANIAH 3:17

Have you heard the Lord your God rejoicing over you? Have you heard Him tell you how wonderful you are, how highly He esteems you? Wouldn't it make you happy to know that your joy in Him is only a shadow of His joy in you?

I'm amazed at how God speaks to me at the unlikeliest times. It's not always while I'm praying, and it's never when I'm trying to be very good or when I'm working myself up into a state of holiness. No, God is more apt to speak while I'm changing my socks, or biting into a big, juicy hamburger, or staring vacantly out the window. In such odd moments the curtain of reality parts and it suddenly dawns on me, "Oh, this is all there is to it? This is all You want of me?"

One day during my experiment, I happened to turn on the radio just as the announcer was introducing a piece of music by John Cage with the odd title "4'33"." I'd heard about this piece but had never heard it performed. Intrigued, I sat down to listen, and I found it to be the most wonderful music I'd ever heard. The pianist who played it began by announcing, "What you are about to hear is exactly what John Cage wanted you to hear. It may not be what you're expecting in a piece of music, but don't adjust your dial. This is the famous piece exactly as John Cage wrote it."

Anyone familiar with this work will be chuckling by now, because what

Cage wrote consists of four minutes and thirty-three seconds of total silence. No, that's not quite accurate. Cage's instructions are for the musicians to pick up their instruments but not to play a note for the entire duration of the piece. So the "music" becomes whatever the listener hears during that time— wind, traffic, birds, people coughing or breathing, nothing at all, or perhaps the sound of blood moving in one's own body.

I listened to this piece mesmerized, because I heard what I can only describe as the sound of the Lord my God rejoicing over me. Though I've heard this before, it always overwhelms me. Recalling other such experiences, I recognize a common thread: It tends to happen when I'm sitting perfectly still, doing nothing.

I have a friend who enjoys just sitting. After years of dreaming about it, he finally started getting up half an hour earlier to make a cup of tea, go out on the porch, and just sit. When I asked him if he prays during this time, he answered, "No, I just sit." He has other times for prayer, but in that first half-hour of the day, he just sits.

Our society has a great need for people who will spend time just sitting. This is the beginning of wonder, and wonder gives birth to joy. Throughout my experiment, again and again the Lord came and restored my joy at times when I was just sitting. He does this all by Himself, without the least effort on my part, quieting me with His love and reminding me that joy is truly miraculous, a work of God.

Though joy may come in many ways, I suspect it may not come at all without attention to this one way of just sitting. To grow a flower, I plant a seed or a bulb. To grow joy, I must plant myself for a while in one place and just sit.

YABBA-KA-DOODLES

Our mouths were filled with laughter,

our tongues with songs of joy.

PSALM 126:2

In a low mood one morning, I set out to have breakfast with my friend Chris Walton. Chris is that rarest of people, someone who always blesses me. No matter what he's going through, what mood he's in, or what we do together, somehow I always leave his company feeling brushed by heavenly light. As we aren't able to see each other often, our times together are all the more precious.

Despite my gloom that day, in Chris's presence I gradually relaxed as we talked about favorite books and music, about our families, and about Jesus. I particularly recall discussing the Jewishness of Jesus, and how during His life the only Bible He had was the Old Testament. The more we talked, the more I sensed a quiet joy tugging at my sleeve like a little child. By the time we rose to leave, though I cannot say I felt entirely happy, a change was stealing over me, a warming. Still, it was the sort of thing that might easily have been snatched away by the next small annoyance, were it not for the strange event that transpired in the parking lot of the restaurant.

We were standing beside our cars, Chris by his door and I by mine, saying our good-byes. Traffic rushed past, making it somewhat difficult to hear our farewells. But as Chris raised his hand in a wave and beamed a last, broad smile, I distinctly heard him call out, "Yabba-ka-doodles!"

Yabba-what? What did he mean? What language was this? As we'd just been talking of Jewish matters, I wondered if Chris might be delivering some traditional Yiddish greeting.

"What did you say?" I called back.

This time Chris threw back his head, beamed as brightly as if he were seeing an angel, and belted out, "YABBA-KA-DOODLES!"

Chris isn't much given to spontaneous ecstatic utterances. Maybe he was
just goofing off? More puzzled than ever, I left my car and walked around to
where he stood.

"I don't get it," I said. "Yabba-ka-doodles. What does it mean?"

"Yabba-what?" said Chris.

"Yabba-ka-doodles. You said Yabba-ka-doodles and I want to know what
it means."

"Yabba-ka-doodles? I didn't say Yabba-ka-doodles."

"Then what did you say?"

"I said, 'I'm glad we could do this.'"

"I'm glad we could do this?" I echoed blankly.

For a moment we stared at one another, listening to the sound of this inane
phrase against the backdrop of the rapturous syllables of *Yabba-ka-doodles*.
And then we burst into laughter, wild, hilarious, thigh-slapping gales of it,
right there in the parking lot. It was so absurd a mistake, so rich and gloriously unlikely. And partly because of that, it filled us with that unlikeliest of
qualities in this darkly unsettling world—JOY!

All the way home in the car I kept muttering, caressing, shouting that
silly word—"Yabba-ka-doodles...yabba-ka-doodles"—giggling and guffaw-
ing like a schoolboy. Talk about joy! More than happy, I felt drunk with joy
for the rest of that day. And when Chris and I next met, we nearly jumped
into each other's arms yelling, "Yabba-ka-doodles, brother!"

Who would have believed that so much joy could be contained in one
crazy, purely imagined word? Later I wondered: Were my ears actually playing tricks, or is it possible that Chris, without realizing it, really did say *Yabba-
ka-doodles?* Was he unknowingly used as a messenger of God to me, delivering
the joyous news of the gospel in an angelic tongue?

PRACTICING THE
PRESENCE OF DOG

You make me glad by your deeds, O LORD;
I sing for joy at the works of your hands.

PSALM 92:4

I cannot write a whole book about joy without mentioning our dog Shelby. Lately it's been raining cats and dogs, and I cannot think of any sight more joyous than that of Shelby bounding through puddles. A medium-sized mutt, she's strong, leggy, fast—and never faster than when raising a glorious spray from mudholes in a rain-soaked meadow. A perfect picture of pure animal joy.

I never wanted Shelby, never wanted a dog. However, my daughter pestered and pestered until eventually she won my wife over, leaving me all alone in my grumblings. After Karen's defection I held out bravely for a few more months, but in my heart I knew the jig was up. Dismally I pictured the endless walks, the chewing and barking, the house full of dog hair, family fights over training and care, the tedious dog-centered conversations with other owners, and worst of all, the poop scooping.

None of these fears has materialized. Shelby is a gentle, loving, obedient dog who fits beautifully into our family. She doesn't bark or chew, I love talking about her, and I'm grateful for the daily walks that get me outside under the wide open sky in all weathers. As for poop scooping, if Shelby does her business near another dog's leavings, I routinely collect both samples.

Having a dog has turned out to be one of the great spiritual experiences of my life. For reasons that date back to childhood, I was cynical about dogs, actually frightened of ever owning one, and Shelby has penetrated these wounds like a healing ointment. Before this I could not have believed the therapeutic power of petting a dog, hugging a dog, talking to a dog, playing tug of war, even letting the dog retrieve balls on the tennis court.

In all sorts of ways Shelby presents me daily, often hourly, with pictures, examples, experiences of joy. If you think I'm exaggerating, you should see the two of us when I pick up her leash and head for the door. At this simple gesture she's consistently so crazily, warm-heartedly enthusiastic, so doggone *grateful,* that I too can't help but be infected with a touch of jubilation. Wouldn't God like to see this same reaction when He does simple things for us? Shouldn't we all be as merry, as good-natured, as appreciative, and as lovingly loyal to our Master as Shelby is?

Every day I thank God for this dog I never wanted. How little I realized that something I was passionately resisting could turn out to be so freeing. Sometimes the pursuit of happiness is like going into a store and trying on hats when a hat is the last thing you think you need. But suddenly you put one on that's perfect—not just perfect but SMASHING! You've never been a hat wearer before but now you are, because this one is absolutely *you,* and despite the outlandish look and the big price tag, you *have* to have it. In the year of my experiment in joy, my biggest surprise was trying on a dog and finding that it fit, and learning that the outside of a dog is good for the inside of a man.

What are you dead set against? Are you sure that thing isn't joy trying to creep up and surprise you? We don't discover joy, it discovers us. It comes bounding into our lives and licks our faces clean to reveal who we are.

SILENT NIGHT,
HOLY WAR

Therefore rejoice, you heavens and you who dwell in them!
But woe to the earth and the sea,
because the devil has gone down to you!
REVELATION 12:12

Day 60 of my experiment happened to fall on Christmas. In all ninety
days I had only four thoroughly unhappy ones—an astonishing
record for me. However, I regret to report that one of my joyless days was
Christmas.

It didn't begin that way. For the first half-hour of Christmas morning,
starting at midnight, I experienced an unusually pure and intense joy accompanied by an almost palpable sense of Jesus' presence. Then, as suddenly as
this began, it was over, and I plunged into the worst night of my entire experiment. All night long I was gripped by the foolish, but very real, fear that I
might not be able to enjoy the next day! Sure enough, I fulfilled the truth of
the saying, "What I fear I create," and Christmas was horrible. Recalling my
experience at midnight, it was almost as if my December 25 recapitulated in
miniature the events of Revelation 12, in which two signs appeared in heaven:
"a woman clothed with the sun" who "was about to give birth," and "an enormous red dragon." When the woman "gave birth to a son, a male child,"
immediately there was "war in heaven" as "Michael and his angels fought
against the dragon" (verses 1-7).

My friend Ron Susek has written a book with the intriguing title *Silent
Night, Holy War.* In this fictional retelling of the Christmas story, Ron

imaginatively weaves together the events of Jesus' birth, as recorded by Matthew and Luke, with the apocalyptic events of Revelation 12. His thesis is that we have every reason to expect Christmas to be a time not only of great joy but also of great struggle and spiritual warfare.[15]

Though we seldom consider this somber side of Christmas, it's nonetheless real. A false god rules over Christmas, manifesting itself as commercialism, busyness, and shallow merriment, making the true Christ as difficult to find now as He was that first Christmas night in a stable in Bethlehem. Yet how many of us approach the birth of the Prince of Peace prepared for conflict?

I, for one, had so looked forward to Christmas being a joyous day, a highlight of my experiment in which I could sing with all my heart, "Joy to the world, the Lord is come!" Perhaps these high expectations were a large part of my problem. With such an attitude, even small annoyances become disproportionately vexing. Joy will not be scheduled. A zealous plan for everything to go smoothly on Christmas Day, or on any day, is a recipe for disaster. Joy lives in the shadow of the cross, not in a Pollyanna world where everything goes well.

I'm reminded of a Christmas card I received, depicting a decorated tree whose shadow, falling across the floor, takes the form of a cross. For Christians the shadow of the cross falls over every day. We live in a spiritual war zone where our enemy the devil observes no holidays but continually "prowls around like a roaring lion looking for someone to devour" (1 Peter 5:8). Why should we expect the road to Christmas to be any easier than the road to Easter? It wasn't easy for Mary or Joseph, or for many others in the original drama. As T. S. Eliot wrote in *Journey of the Magi*, "This Birth was / Hard and bitter agony for us, like Death, our death."[16]

Christ doesn't come to our righteousness but to our unrighteousness. He doesn't come to our airbrushed fantasies but into the heart of our real pain. Indeed if we do not let Him into our pain, we will not experience His coming, or His joy, at all.

GLAD TIDINGS

Do not be afraid. I bring you good news of great joy
that will be for all the people.

LUKE 2:10

Christmas that year was foggy. For five days without a break our city was thickly shrouded. Rudolph had his work cut out for him. The day after Christmas we planned to leave our balmy coastal climate and drive for seven hours to a frozen lake in the interior of British Columbia, to spend a week in a tiny cabin with no running water or electricity. Just snow, ice, stars, silence, and our small family.

As we prepared for our journey, I wasn't looking forward to a long drive through spectacular scenery in the fog. So we prayed. Just before backing the car out of the driveway, we asked God for sunshine. In one of the quickest, most dramatic answers to prayer I've ever seen, by the time we drove one block up the street, the five-day fog entirely lifted, and we enjoyed a beautiful trip.

Throughout that week God continued to pierce various kinds of mist with the sunshine of His joy. That same day, stuck in snow on a secondary road, I had occasion to use tire chains for the first time in my life. I was amazed at how those chains instantly gripped the snowy road and we took off. In the same way, I thought, joy grips life. Feeling stuck? Spinning your wheels? Put on some joy. Joy bites into life with enthusiasm, taking firm hold and moving one forward in all conditions.

Because our cabin had no running water, every morning I hauled water in pails from the lake, first breaking the skin of ice with an axe. This hardy ritual brought me great joy. Each time I took up the axe I thought of Franz

Kafka's famous words: "A book must be an ice-axe to break the sea frozen inside us," for if it's not, "why then do we read it?"[17] Similarly we might ask: If the life we're leading isn't happy, why not drop everything right now and pursue joy at any cost?

Each day at the lake I'd take a chair out onto the ice and sit for a while, basking in the white, majestic serenity of this place. It was so quiet I could strain my ears and still hear no sound at all. For a person used to the city, such perfect stillness can be unnerving; it exaggerates every little noise within one-self. Most of these quiet times on the ice I thoroughly enjoyed, but one day the utter silence and emptiness of the landscape got to me. I actually grew frightened, spooked to the point that I picked up my chair and was heading back to the cabin when suddenly, for the first and only time that day, the sun came out. It didn't shine for long through the thick cloud cover, just enough to poke one strong, warm ray into the center of my heart. Immediately I felt different, warmed through and through and filled with joy. So I sat down in my chair again to praise the Lord.

That one ray of sunshine preached to me the message of Christmas—how the Son of God came into the world to dispel the wintry clouds of our fear and to warm our hearts with His astonishing love. The entire spiritual history of humanity can be traced in my movement that day from one chair position to another—from cold dread at the eerie, empty majesty of nature to the personal warmth of an intimate Savior-God breaking into history to announce, "Don't be afraid! I love you and bring tidings of fantastic joy!"

TENDING THE FIRE

Never be lacking in zeal, but keep your spiritual fervor,
serving the Lord. Be joyful in hope.

ROMANS 12:11-12

During our week in a remote cabin, our only source of heat was a wood-burning stove. There's an art to building a fire that will warm a cabin for an entire winter's night. The first night my fire went out, and I had to get up at three o'clock to rebuild it. By the time I crept back to bed, I was wide awake and freezing. Even with a roaring fire, a cold cabin warms slowly, so I had lots of time to lie there shivering and wondering if I was having fun yet.

As I prayed, however, the Lord built a fire in me. I could feel Him doing it, could feel the warmth of His Spirit percolating through the cold cabin of my soul. It took a long time for God's fire to warm me all the way through, but eventually it did. Seldom have I felt so clearly the stark contrast between the Spirit's fire and the cold, dead ashes of the flesh.

Throughout our week at the lake, tending the fire became a symbol to me of the spiritual life, and especially of joy. In the dead of winter in a frozen wilderness, to keep a fire lit requires setting aside all else whenever the fire falters and doing whatever it takes to rebuild it. When the fire in our cabin fizzled out, I didn't want to be bothered with it, but I had to bother or else freeze. I knew that with a little skill, dedication, and work, we'd soon be warm again. Meanwhile my ninety-day experiment was teaching me that the same is true of joy. Yes, joy is God's gift, but we must stretch out our hands to split the kindling of prayer, carry the logs of good deeds, lay the fire of faith, and strike the match of the Spirit. If we do our part, the Lord will not fail to build a cheerful, roaring fire in our hearts.

This book isn't just about lighting our fire but about making it blaze—bright enough to put a twinkle in the eyes and a spring in the step, cozy enough to warm others, dazzling enough to set the world on fire. Every day we take pains to look after our physical needs—food, sleep, clothes, housing. Why won't we approach spiritual needs with this same urgency? In our country we have no shortage of fuel to heat our homes, yet often our spirits remain cold. Has the devil convinced us there's not enough joy of the Lord to go around?

In the Old Testament the Lord appeared to Moses in a bush that was on fire but "did not burn up" (Exodus 3:2). A similar phenomenon appeared in the New Testament, but this time the fire was on people: "They saw what seemed to be tongues of fire that separated and came to rest on each of them" (Acts 2:3). Two disciples who met the resurrected Jesus asked, "Were not our hearts burning within us while he talked with us?" (Luke 24:32). Human hearts are meant for burning, but we have two choices of how to burn—consumed with selfishness or warmed with the joy of the Lord.

Tending the fire of joy in our hearts is really no more difficult than maintaining a wood fire in an uninsulated, ramshackle cabin. All it takes is a little skill and a sense of urgency. The fire comes from God, but we must provide faith, work, and fuel. Anyone can learn to do this if it's important enough. Are you cold enough yet? When it's important to be warm in your cabin, you'll find a way to light the fire.

A CONTINUAL FEAST

All the days of the oppressed are wretched,

but the cheerful heart has a continual feast.

PROVERBS 15:15

M ost people have at least one big problem standing in the way of their happiness. What is it for you? A chronic illness? A troubled marriage? No marriage? Wild kids? Financial worries? A crummy job? Probably you think that if only you could solve this one problem (and maybe a few others), then you'd be happy. Right?

Wrong. If you managed to solve your one big problem, another would rush in to take its place. Then another and another. This is how it goes with problems. There's no end to them. The real problem is that you think you cannot be happy as long as you have a problem. You'll always have problems; therefore you'll never be happy.

The solution to this pitiful dilemma is easy: First become happy, and then you'll be able to handle your problems. Happiness holds tremendous power for creating good. Rather than thinking that you cannot rejoice because of all that's wrong, take hold of joy to celebrate all that's right, and so overcome the wrong. Who benefits from your frowns and your artificial smiles? Think of all the praise you've withheld from God because you cannot quite bring yourself to believe that a gracious heavenly Father wants you, His little child, to lift your face to the light and be happy with Him, starting now.

"But so many terrible things have happened to me," you groan. "I need to work through all this before I can be happy." No, this is a lie. The devil would like to keep you working all your life and never have a moment's contentment. The time to get off the treadmill is now. Christian life is eternal life, and the eternal starts now. "Now is the time of God's favor, now is the day of salvation" (2 Corinthians 6:2). If you're unhappy now, don't fret or feel guilty about it. Guilt and worry only perpetuate misery. Instead, be happy. Change your mind about the outrageous impracticality of this advice. If the Bible says "Rejoice always," there must be something to it.

But you object: "I can't be happy, because I'm sick," or "I can't be happy, because my husband has left me," or "I can't be happy, because I'm sad." Don't you understand? Happiness is the very weapon you need to surmount all these conditions. Happiness doesn't come to those who sit around waiting until life gets better. Happiness comes to those who grab hold of its proffered hand in order to rise up and conquer their struggles.

The one prerequisite for happiness is the acceptance of whatever is. Am I overtired? Fine. Sick? Very well, then. Unemployed? Okay, I'll work with that. To accept what is doesn't mean I do not try to change what is. All change, however, begins with acceptance. I cannot change or heal what I do not acknowledge.

We're so sure we'd be happy if only we could get free of our troubles, but going through life without troubles is not an option. While trouble-free times may come, at best they endure briefly, and they may even create a false sense of security. As it turns out, being happy has nothing to do with having trouble or not having it. Rather it's one's attitude toward trouble that makes all the difference.

Life is full of problems. Learn to be happy in spite of them, because they aren't going away. Yes, many will go away, but only to be replaced by other problems. Be happy with the problems you have, because the ones that are coming may be worse. Meanwhile the feast of life has been prepared just for you. Sit down and enjoy.

IS LIFE FAIR?

He has shown kindness by giving you rain from heaven
and crops in their seasons; he provides you with plenty of food
and fills your hearts with joy.

ACTS 14:17

P aul speaks these words to a crowd of pagans. If God gives joy and other good things to unbelievers, how much more will He do so for His own dear children!

I'm convinced that what keeps us from a joy-filled life is a lingering resentment of God, a latent conviction that God isn't fair and that life is too hard. When a difficult situation arises, don't we fall apart because we sincerely believe it's too hard not to? Don't we secretly see life as an exam that keeps throwing questions at us for which we haven't been prepared and to which there are no good answers? If this happened in any school or university, we'd have good reason to sue the administration. Since we don't know how to complain against God, our frustrations fester, robbing us of joy.

What to do? Make up your mind once and for all that this is God's exam and He can pose any questions He likes, and all of them are fair. Don't just accept this as a propositional truth, but *feel* the truth of it. Stop believing the fashionable heresy that life is unfair. Life *is* fair. It's fair in the ultimate sense, the only sense that counts, for "the LORD works righteousness and justice for all the oppressed" (Psalm 103:6). More than fair, life is a pure and perfect gift that continually invites us to joy in its staggering richness.

Resentment of God is the main reason the world does not accept Jesus. It's easy to blame God for all our problems, but it's more difficult to blame Jesus, who is so obviously good, innocent, and just. Even non-Christian religions reserve a place of honor for Jesus because they know, as the thief at Calvary confessed, "This man has done nothing wrong" (Luke 23:41). Jesus Himself challenged, "Can any of you prove me guilty of sin?" (John 8:46). No, we can't, and so instead we turn our suspicions upon God. Jesus has a human face, but God we can hold at arm's length as an abstraction and pile on the blame.

The Christian, however, knows that Jesus, not some abstraction, is God. Jesus is "the radiance of God's glory and the exact representation of his being" (Hebrews 1:3). Whatever we see in Jesus, we can trust that God is just the same. For example, many persist in believing that sickness and affliction are necessarily God's doing, but Jesus, far from causing anyone harm, "went around doing good and healing all who were under the power of the devil" (Acts 10:38). This is the truth about God. To be a Christian is to let Jesus correct our theology and lead us to His Father, "the God of all comfort" (2 Corinthians 1:3).

When I first began my experiment in joy, I thought I was doing something quite radical. Now I see that for a true disciple, giving up quarrelling, rising above despair, resolving to trust and hope in all circumstances is all in the ordinary line of duty. There's nothing heroic here, nothing above and beyond. The result—abiding joy—is what every follower of Jesus should be experiencing normally. All that holds us back is the pitifully compromised state of our Christianity and our own stubborn resentment of God. How we'd love to prove God wrong! Yet Scripture insists, "Let God be true, and every man a liar" (Romans 3:4).

No wonder we're unhappy if we're setting ourselves on the throne of the universe in place of God. To take up the cross is to get down off our throne.

CARPE DIEM

Be happy, young man, while you are young,
and let your heart give you joy in the days of your youth.
ECCLESIASTES 11:9

Christian tradition holds an ancient distinction between two ways of spirituality, one called the *via negativa* (the negative, or apophatic, way) and the other the *via affirmativa* (the affirmative, or kataphatic, way). At the risk of oversimplifying these two paths, we can say that the apophatic disciple makes progress by mourning the absence of God, whereas the kataphatic disciple celebrates the presence of God. The negative path stresses the purgation of all the appetites, both sensual and spiritual, while the affirmative path is devoted to the full enjoyment of everything good.

While there's joy in both these ways, when the follower of the via negativa experiences joy he says, "This is only a faint picture of what's to come," whereas the affirmer smiles from ear to ear and fully relishes his joy. The former, desiring God alone above all else, shuns personal happiness, knowing it's less than God. The latter, also desiring God alone above all else, gladly embraces happiness, knowing it is God's good gift. Where the via negativa says "Deny yourself," the via affirmativa cries *"Carpe diem":* Seize the day and squeeze all the joy you can from it. One way eschews pleasure because it's fleeting; the other celebrates every passing moment precisely because it's fleeting and will never come again.

Which is your way? For many years I tried to follow the via negativa, partly because I saw it as more holy, but mostly because the via affirmativa seemed to go against the grain of my naturally moody temperament. I did not possess the strength of soul to celebrate life vigorously. While I had times of joyous living, I could not sustain joy as a lifestyle. I wanted to, but it seemed too much work. I thought of myself as going through a long "desert experience," when really I was just depressed.

Depression and the spiritual desert are not the same. In the Bible the Israelites wandered for forty years in the wilderness, not because they were following the via negativa but because of disobedience. Far from maturing spiritually in the desert, they died there without ever gaining the promises of God. Jesus too spent time in the desert, but He didn't get stuck there wandering around. He went for a limited time, propelled by the Holy Spirit, for the specific purpose of confronting the enemy. While it's tempting to spiritualize the desert, the Bible teaches that it's no place to settle down.

In retrospect I see my relationship with the via negativa as an ill-fitting coat. When eventually I came to understand the via affirmativa enough to adopt it, I felt I'd finally put on the coat that was right for me. The Bible encourages us to "put on the new self, created to be like God in true righteousness and holiness" (Ephesians 4:24). Joy, an aspect of the new self, comes from wearing the right coat.

Be careful of the via negativa; it's a path to which few are truly called. However, anyone can be an affirmer of life's goodness. Anyone can begin right now to rejoice in the Lord. As you open your curtains each morning, what's the look on your face? That look has much to do with determining the character of your entire day. Why not put on a smile as part of your carefully selected wardrobe? Joy begins in the morning with getting up on the right side of the bed. It continues with buttering your toast on the right side, staying on the right side of your spouse, adopting the right attitude toward your work, and walking on the sunny side of the street wherever you go. There's a right side to everything, and that's where joy is found.

NEXT!

Forgetting what is behind and straining toward what is ahead,
I press on toward the goal to win the prize
for which God has called me heavenward in Christ Jesus.

PHILIPPIANS 3:13-14

To seize joy in the present, it's necessary to forget what's behind. A whole day can be lost in ruing what happened the day before. An afternoon can disappear under the weight of one chance event of the morning. A picayune mistake, or even just a perceived mistake, can entirely overshadow an otherwise wonderful experience. I have a friend who, when overtaken by that terrible sense of "oh-no-what-have-I-done," likes to toss the whole mess over her shoulder and say, "Next!" In this way she's ready for whatever comes.

God says the same: "Forget the former things; do not dwell on the past. See, I am doing a new thing! Now it springs up; do you not perceive it?" (Isaiah 43:18-19). We won't perceive the new if we're busy living in the past. It's enough to tackle today's problems without rehashing yesterday's. "Each day has enough trouble of its own" (Matthew 6:34).

Of course we don't forget the past entirely. Much joy comes from reliving past happiness and also from working through former pain. However, so much energy can be spent processing ancient history that nothing is left for assimilating today's good, let alone for "straining toward what is ahead."

Joy requires optimism—optimism not only about the future but about the past. The worse our past has been, the more need we have to be optimistic about it. Forgiveness means letting go of the hope of a better past. Optimism, like forgiveness, reaches into yesterday and actually changes what we thought could never be changed. The terrible blunder we made last week suddenly becomes a blessing, a doorway into some new opportunity. Just as regret over yesterday has the power to spoil today, so joy today has the power to obliterate a lifetime of pain. Is such joy an illusion? No, it's the truth, but it takes optimism to see this. Where there's been much pain, the Lord will give much joy to more than make up for "the years the locusts have eaten" (Joel 2:25).

I once heard someone described as being "optimistic to the core." This phrase strikes me as expressing the true goal of my experiment in joy—not necessarily to feel joyful at every moment, but rather to be always optimistic. For the optimist every problem is an opportunity to take optimism deeper, closer to the core. Where formerly it seemed that nothing could lift us out of the mire, optimism brings us to the point where nothing can alienate our happiness.

Some book titles are unforgettable. One such title for me has been Robert Brow's *Living Totally Without Guilt*.[18] Often in times of stress I'll murmur this phrase, extracting its secret like juice from a pomegranate. While it's sometimes appropriate for a Christian to feel guilt, we've no need to live there. When people sinned in the Old Testament, they had to go to the temple and wait for a priest to perform a sacrifice to free them from guilt. As Christians we no longer have to wait, not even for one minute, for "one greater than the temple is here" (Matthew 12:6). No more messing with bloody carcasses; in the temple of our own minds and bodies, where the Holy Spirit dwells, we can instantly hand the whole mess over to Jesus. The happy person is not the one who sets out to be joyful and achieves success, but the one who looks his failures in the eye and then tosses them over his shoulder, saying, "Next!"

CHAMPAGNE OF CANA

Go, eat your food with gladness,
and drink your wine with a joyful heart,
for it is now that God favors what you do.

ECCLESIASTES 9:7

Day 67 of my experiment fell on January 1, 2000, widely celebrated as the dawn of the new millennium. That New Year's Eve we sat with friends around a campfire beside a frozen lake in the interior of British Columbia. At midnight we watched in wonder as bursts of fireworks, dramatically illuminating the falling snow, flowered in the vast, dark whiteness.

On the stroke of twelve we toasted the new millennium with a bottle of sparkling apple juice, and I had what I can only describe as a mystical experience. As I raised the glass to my lips and drank, I felt I had never before tasted anything so delicious. The juice was like an ambrosial nectar, exquisitely refreshing, even intoxicating (though it contained no alcohol). It was as if that bottle contained the very essence of my surroundings on that unique night— the dark frozen wilderness, the bright falling snow, the bursting fireworks, the cool bite of winter in the air, the gentle warmth of friends around a campfire. Mix all these together in a drink, along with a hint of something exotic and unnameable, and the taste came as near as I can imagine to the taste of joy itself—truly a champagne for the soul.

Joy filled me that night, and again in the morning upon awakening to a world of sparkling whiteness. The whole lake was covered in a blanket of clean new snow, not a mark on it. This beautiful symbol of a brand-new millennium was matched by a feeling of clean freshness and limitless possibility in my own spirit. Perhaps this is the pinnacle of earthly joy—this sensation of pure oneness with one's surroundings, of complete harmony between inner and outer worlds.

A similar sense of mystical oneness with the physical world came over me many times during my experiment in joy. Sometimes joy came through contemplating spiritual truths or through overcoming problems of an abstract nature. Just as often, however, I found the vehicle of joy was something thoroughly physical—a painting, a piece of music, a flower, a hug or a touch, a drink of sparkling apple juice. At times I might seem to derive nothing from an hour of prayer, only to go outside and discover the joy of the Lord in the wind on my face. Often I sat down to meals that seemed the best I'd ever eaten. Yes, there were good friends around the table and many spiritual reasons to be happy, yet it wouldn't have been the same without the physical presence of roast beef and gravy, Yorkshire pudding, peas and yams, golden brown potatoes, and chocolate cupcakes. Nehemiah knew this when he told his people, "Go and enjoy choice food and sweet drinks...for the joy of the LORD is your strength" (8:10).

To the Christian, the physical and the spiritual are not separate but complementary. To be spiritually alive and happy is to find the physical senses awakening as never before. Nothing is more physical than the incarnation, death, resurrection, and ascension of Jesus. Because our awesome Creator God made this world with His own hands and further hallowed it by living here Himself, joy is free to take full delight in earthly existence, fleeting though it may be—just as Jesus did when He turned water into wine at a wedding feast. If ever any drink was more delicious than the one I tasted that New Year's Eve, surely it was the champagne of Cana with which Jesus inaugurated the kingdom of heaven.

AIR SANDWICHES

Those who hope in the LORD will renew their strength.
They will soar on wings like eagles;
they will run and not grow weary,
they will walk and not be faint.

ISAIAH 40:31

It's tempting to read Isaiah's words as a message about deferred joy. To "hope in the LORD" can be construed to mean that we aren't happy now but we will be if only we wait and hope. However, the line about walking without fainting casts doubt on this interpretation. Yes, sometimes we'll joyfully "soar on wings like eagles," and any long-distance runner knows the euphoria of running without weariness. However, a quiet, undramatic joy will also pervade the daily walk of those who wait on the Lord. Waiting, it turns out, is a joyful activity in itself. It's possible to know the luminous uplift of the Spirit in all of life's situations from the high to the low, from the dramatic to the mundane.

I hadn't traveled far in my ninety-day experiment before the novelty of my adventure began to wear thin. By the second week the sameness of daily life had set in, and by the third month this dailiness was even more telling. It was January, a traditionally low month, and my outward life seemed almost dull—yet still I remained joyful. As I examined the reasons for my joy in the midst of the most ordinary days, I realized that joy loves ordinary life best of all. Joy thrives on what all the rest of the world overlooks. The smaller, the plainer, the more lowly the circumstances, the happier joy is.

Of course joy can also thrive in exotic and thrilling situations. Joy itself does not inhere, however, in the exotic and the thrilling, which are rare, but in the ordinary which is everywhere. As I ride a roller coaster with my daughter, what produces joy is not the roller coaster but the fact of sharing an experience with my daughter, which I could also do at home. Or maybe it's watching the people in the car ahead that brings me joy, or noticing the way the sun shines on the rooftops around. Without the enjoyment of such ordinary things, a roller-coaster ride falls flat.

Those who think of joy as flashy and exciting will also find it fickle, for not much of life is glitzy. True joy, far from being loud and capricious, is by nature just the opposite—quiet and faithful. The joy of the Lord is so dependable that it remains when all else falls to pieces. Elijah learned this as he huddled in the cave at Horeb and heard the voice of the Lord, not in wind or earthquake or fire, but in "a gentle whisper" (1 Kings 19:12)—the reminder of joy's fidelity in a time of deep discouragement.

Joy loves the ordinary, the unnoticed, the unassuming in life. Indeed joy loves nothing best of all. When nothing is happening, then joy can be happiest. I'm reminded of a character called the Snitznoodle in the Raggedy Ann books by Johnny Gruelle, which were favorites of mine as a child. This fellow lived on air sandwiches. To make an air sandwich, you place the palm of one hand above the palm of the other hand, a few inches apart according to taste, and then you move the slab to your mouth and take a big bite. Air sandwiches are quite handy when there's nothing else to eat.

This is the food of joy.

NO RECIPE

The time is short. From now on
those who have wives should live as if they had none;
those who mourn, as if they did not;
those who are happy, as if they were not.

1 CORINTHIANS 7:29-30

The passage above is full of surprises. Why in the world would Paul advise people who are happy to live "as if they were not"?

Like Paul, I find it necessary to contradict myself right and left in this book. One day joy happens one way, the next it happens entirely differently. One night I lie awake crying out to God and no answer comes. The next morning, hung over with fatigue, I resign myself to a thoroughly miserable day, when suddenly God floods me with joy.

Who can make sense of this? There's no recipe for joy, no surefire technique for procuring it. If I'm trying to be happy today in the same way I was happy yesterday, I'll fail. The manna of joy falls in limitless supply, but each day's rations must be gathered afresh. Joy inhabits only the present moment; if I can't embrace it now, it's gone.

What keeps me from seizing joy in the moment? Sorrow, obviously; yet joy too, either remembered or anticipated, can alienate me from present reality. Great things have happened and will happen, but they cannot compare with what God does right now, that His power and glory may continually spring forth fresh.

Like the play of sunlight on water, joy shifts from moment to moment. Wild and free, scornful of rules, joy refuses to be pinned down and systematized in a book. Joy is not something to be written or read about, but lived.

It does not exist on paper but only in real life. As an author the best I can do is to point to joy breathlessly, as to a shooting star, and cry out, "Wow! Look at that!" Like a physicist trying to catch some ephemeral nuclear particle in the laboratory, I can only examine the traces left behind by joy's fiery passage.

Joy is shy; it doesn't like to be spied on. Sadness will hold your gaze as happiness never will. Depression can last and last without one's lifting a finger, but not joy. The kind of joy that lasts is like a big lake trout, still and camouflaged, inhabiting the deep, shadowed places of the heart. You know it's there, but thrust your hand into the water to touch it, and it's gone. You're blessed just to catch a glimpse of joy, let alone lay it out on the table and write a whole book about it.

During my experiment, while I seldom grew tired of seeking joy, I did grow tired of thinking and writing about it. I longed not to study joy but simply to enjoy it. Often I was tempted to abandon any thought of writing a book; I kept on only because I had an assignment from the Lord. What wearied me was not joy itself but constantly observing joy, a process that easily gets in the way of the phenomenon itself. Joy shrinks from being gazed at, because it's a product of gazing elsewhere. Joy finds its center not in itself but in others, above all in God. Rather than talking about itself, joy prefers to talk of what—and especially of who—it loves. Locate the meaning of joy in itself, and it shrivels up.

For this reason Paul advises "those who are happy" not to cling to being happy but to live "as if they were not"—the same advice he extends to "those who mourn." Somehow true joy is to be found between these two extremes, neither indulging in melancholy nor overindulging in happiness.

NEW EYES

The eye is the lamp of the body. If your eyes are good,
your whole body will be full of light.

MATTHEW 6:22

J oy arises from right understanding. It's really a matter of how one looks at things. The further I traveled in my experiment, the more I realized I was undergoing a conversion in my understanding, a change in my way of looking at the world and at my own life. I was beginning to see with new eyes. Everything I looked at and thought about was bathed in the light of joy. It was as if I'd lived in shade all my life, and suddenly the sun came out. When the sun shines, it shines on everything. Even shadows serve only to make the sunlight more beautiful.

One day as I walked to the mailbox, my eye fastened on one pink rosebud just beginning to blossom. I stopped and studied it for a long time, drinking in its simple beauty. Though the day was dismal and drizzly, this flower seemed to glow with a light of its own. A patina of tiny silver raindrops made it shine all the brighter.

How simple and available are the springs of joy! Later that day when I came to write about what had brought me the most joy, it was this flower. Thinking about my little rosebud all through the day, and then writing about it, increased my joy. Even now as I recall it, joy returns.

"Consider how the lilies grow," said Jesus. "They do not labor or spin" (Luke 12:27). Is your life full of labor and spinning in circles? Try taking a good long look at a flower, and consider how simply and naturally life can be lived.

As I pondered the wondrous beauty of my one flower, it came to represent for me the whole kingdom of God as it reigns even now in the midst of this dark world. Everywhere, if I have eyes to see, bloom obvious signs of God's glory. One day "the earth will be filled with the knowledge of the glory of the LORD, as the waters cover the sea" (Habakkuk 2:14). As I look with new eyes, I see this glory now. Already I can see "the new Jerusalem, coming down out of heaven from God, prepared as a bride beautifully dressed for her husband" (Revelation 21:2). I won't see this if I look at the world with a skeptical, jaded understanding. Yet if I look with the eyes of joy, between here and the mailbox I'll find a hundred reasons to celebrate the fact that I live already in the kingdom of God.

This kingdom, teaches Paul, "is not a matter of eating and drinking, but of righteousness, peace and joy in the Holy Spirit" (Romans 14:17). Often we get sidetracked and let insignificant matters eclipse what is most important. Forgetting that the kingdom of God is fundamentally about peace and joy, we act as if it's really about work, doing our duty, making enough money, building the church, organizing prayer meetings, or keeping other Christians in line. Why do we find it so hard to believe that joy is at the center, not at the periphery, of the spiritual life? Joy is what gives the spark to everything else. With joy we can accomplish much work; without joy we can work and work and get nowhere.

Joy is a pure, sweet fruit of the Holy Spirit, and simplicity is its hallmark. One recognizes the real thing by its untainted purity. Joy will not compete for long with doubts, denials, excuses, compromises. Either the doubts must go, or joy goes. Joy wants all or nothing. Joy is bent on covering the whole earth with the glory of God.

THE LANGUAGE OF LOVE

These I will bring to my holy mountain
and give them joy in my house of prayer.

ISAIAH 56:7

Whenever the above verse is quoted, usually we hear only the second half: "My house will be called a house of prayer for all nations." We miss the fact that the house of prayer is meant to be full of joy. Jesus quoted this verse in Mark 11:17 when He chased the moneychangers out of the temple. Beneath His angry violence, His motive was to bring joy.

Joy and prayer belong together. Paul thought so when he wrote, "Be joyful always; pray continually; give thanks in all circumstances, for this is God's will for you in Christ Jesus" (1 Thessalonians 5:16-18). Many Christians have wondered how it's possible to "pray continually," but not many notice the words immediately preceding: "Be joyful always." We're more familiar with the call to prayer than with the call to joy. We know the saying, "God loves a cheerful giver" (2 Corinthians 9:7), but do we realize He also loves a cheerful pray-er?

Many avoid prayer because they find no joy in it. They find no joy because they either ritualize the life out of prayer, turning it into something they cannot bear, or else squeeze it into such cramped spaces that it feels like a wolfed breakfast rather than a relaxed, candlelit dinner. Prayer is the language of love, of intimate relationship. Give up on trying to impress the boss. When you're with a lover, do what you love. If listening to music helps you pray, do that. If you need to be outside, go outside. If you enjoy hot baths, have one. Do whatever works to relax you enough for love.

There are many ways to pray, and most of us try every way except the one that brings real joy. Dutiful, joyless prayer is of no value. It would be better to quit such prayer altogether and go in search of joy. Look for joy, and true prayer will find you.

Better still, pray for joy. James wrote, "You do not have, because you do not ask God" (4:2). In the Lord's Prayer we ask for our daily bread; similarly we must ask regularly for joy, as David did: "Bring joy to your servant, for to you, O Lord, I lift up my soul" (Psalm 86:4). The prayer of asking is a powerful prayer, for it puts complete faith in God as the sole source of all goodness. Of course something I've done, or left undone, may be blocking my joy, and then the initiative to act lies with me. More often, however, when I ask God for joy, it simply comes, sometimes immediately. Throughout my experiment I saw this happen again and again.

Living with joy could be compared to a little boy driving a powerful speedboat. For a while your dad lets you drive all by yourself and it's thrilling, but before long, problems arise: Dangerous shoals loom, weeds tangle in the propeller, or maybe you just get tired or start to doubt yourself. Help! And help is always close at hand. All you have to do is say, "Daddy, would You please take the wheel again?"

Words are not important in prayer. Prayer isn't about words but about a true turning of the heart toward the Lord. You may say a lot of words or meditate a great deal and get nowhere, but when you turn your heart to God in sincere expectancy, He surely answers. At times I'm so weary or burdened that it's all I can do simply to look to Him, but this is enough. This is everything. Without this simple looking to the Lord, there is no prayer, no joy.

LAVISH WORSHIP

God has ascended amid shouts of joy,
the LORD amid the sounding of trumpets.

PSALM 47:5

The key to Psalm 47, a tremendous hymn of enthronement, is that it recalls the occasion when David "danced before the LORD with all his might, while he and the entire house of Israel brought up the ark of the LORD with shouts and the sound of trumpets" (2 Samuel 6:14-15). What a celebration took place as the earthly habitation of God was brought for the first time into the city of Jerusalem, its proper resting place. The psalm commemorates the establishment of God in His rightful place and foresees the time when the Lord will be enthroned, not just over one city or one people, but over all—"For God is the King of all the earth" (verse 7).

Meanwhile another kind of enthronement takes place for each individual who installs the Lord as King in his own heart. As we enthrone the Lord, shouts of joy will be released, for joy is the spontaneous result of exalting the Lord as King. More than an appropriate accompaniment to worship, joy is a mark of the real thing. Joy comes from giving God His rightful place.

True worship doesn't depend on words, music, or rituals, but is an inward turning of the heart to the Lord in adoration. Accordingly, worship doesn't require a special time or place, but is something that can and should be done anywhere and everywhere, all day long. "Blessed are those who dwell in your house; they are ever praising you" (Psalm 84:4). Worship is a place to stay, a way of thinking and being in all circumstances. As we live in worship, joy accompanies us.

This isn't as complicated as it may sound. Rather, it's the natural result of knowing the Lord as He is. If I do not worship God readily and lavishly, I'm overlooking who He is and all His blessings. Whenever I actually notice His majesty and His bountiful love, I *will* worship—I won't be able to stop myself! Worship is the attitude of someone who is not just following Jesus but chasing after Him. If you knew He was passing along your street right now, wouldn't you run outside to see Him? People who are deeply happy are not just walking but running to meet God. They're excited!

When I feel dull or grumpy, I throw myself at the feet of Jesus until gradually (or sometimes suddenly) He fills me with His glory and joy. In this way I see the direct connection between worship and joy. How could joy *not* issue from entering into the presence of such a glorious and intimate God? Joy does not always flow immediately from worship, but it does flow inevitably. Often in the middle of a sleepless night I've turned my heart persistently to Almighty God and felt no instant relief, but then awakened to joy in the morning.

If we lack joy, it's because some measure of doubt keeps us from worshiping our King wholeheartedly. If only we trust Him with everything we have and are, joy will be ours. Happiness is no path for the halfhearted. Unless we're prepared to give our whole being to the God of joy, happiness will elude us. When we do give ourselves unrestrainedly, the floodgates of joy fly open, for true worship evokes a response. Joy is God's rejoinder to our heartfelt adoration of Him.

LET'S CELEBRATE!

There will be more rejoicing in heaven over one sinner
who repents than over ninety-nine righteous persons
who do not need to repent.

LUKE 15:7

At first sight there seems something not quite right about this verse. As wonderful as it is to see new converts to Christ, don't we old, righteous believers make God just as happy as the new ones?

No. In fact, God gets a bigger bang out of the new ones, and so should we. As long as we insist on making joy revolve around ourselves, we'll be less than happy. True joy is centered in God—in His gospel, His character, His passions. To know the joy of the Lord is to align ourselves with what gladdens His heart. Scripture says plainly that God is happier about new believers than old ones. Let's get with the program.

One evening, drained after a busy day, I'd just sat down for a few quiet moments of spiritual reading. When the doorbell rang, I groaned. From my study on the top floor I listened resentfully to the sound of my wife welcoming unexpected guests. I soon gathered that a woman we'd known for ten years, who seemed chronically unlucky in love, had just arrived with her new boyfriend. Having not the slightest desire to meet this fellow, I furiously immersed myself in my book, refusing even to respond when my wife called me. *She invited them in,* I thought bitterly, *so she can entertain them.* Finally my daughter, a feisty soul, barged into my study and physically yanked me out of my chair and dragged me downstairs.

Upon entering the living room, I thrust out my hand to the stranger and blurted out, "So tell me, what do you think of Jesus Christ?" I'm not usually so aggressive in personal evangelism, but having been rudely roused from my study, I felt mean as a bear. If I had to visit with people, I was determined to mince no words.

For the next three hours this fellow joined me in the most exciting dialogue about faith. By the end of the evening I had him backed squarely against the wall, yet still he wouldn't cave in. He didn't become a Christian that night, but shortly afterward he had a powerful encounter with Jesus in a vision, and finally he surrendered.

What joy this gave me! I definitely felt swept up in the party going on in heaven. The one thing better than being in the kingdom myself is seeing someone else arrive. Every second, somewhere in the world, someone turns to Christ. Is this alone not cause for continual rejoicing? What good is it for new people to keep flocking into the kingdom if we old ones aren't happy there?

In Luke 15 Jesus tells three parables of repentant sinners, and at the end of each we're invited to rejoice. The shepherd announces, "Rejoice with me; I have found my lost sheep" (verse 6); the woman exclaims, "Rejoice with me; I have found my lost coin" (verse 9); the father of the prodigal crows, "Let's have a feast and celebrate" (verse 23). At the heart of the kingdom of heaven, a celebration is going on. What's the occasion? It's not that all wars are over, or all suffering ended, or all the world converted. No, the occasion is that one lost sheep has come home. Joy, overlooking all the good reasons for pessimism, throws a big party over one lovely flower, one bird call, one child's smile, one earth-shattering change in a human heart. How about leaving our somber studies to join the revelry of angels?

JOYFUL NOISE

O come, let us sing unto the LORD;
let us make a joyful noise to the rock of our salvation.

PSALM 95:1 (KJV)

I'm not fond of machines. I don't like their noise or what they do to the environment. Right this moment one of the noisiest of all machines, a leaf blower, is destroying the peace of my neighborhood. I rejoiced when I heard about an organization seeking to ban leaf blowers. Often I wish I'd lived in a period before the advent of machines, especially loud stereos.

Nevertheless, I'm a child of the modern age and I must live with machines. Machines have helped to build my house and to prepare my food, and other machines carry me long distances to visit people I love. I recognize that machines do me much good, yet still I find it difficult to feel warmly toward them.

During my experiment, a huge construction site sprang up overnight on a quiet street where I like to walk. Seeing a mammoth crane blocking my path one day, my first impulse was that of the Pharisee: cross to the other side of the road. Instead, under a peculiar inspiration, I kept straight on. Like a man deliberately walking under a ladder I passed right beneath the boom of that crane, smiled broadly up at the operator, and drank in the full brouhaha of the roaring engine. Then I went on my way singing a joyful song.

This was a small incident, but my action held a large and specific meaning for me. Some months earlier I'd sat with a friend in an espresso shop, when for some reason he told me a secret that he'd never shared with anyone except his wife. After checking over his shoulder, he leaned close to me and said in a low voice, "I like to sing with machines."

"You what?"

"I sing with machines. I know it sounds silly, but there it is."

My friend then explained that every machine, however noisy, has a musical pitch with accompanying harmonics. One can create music by zeroing in on this pitch and embroidering a melody around it.

Intrigued, I asked for a demonstration. Just then an espresso machine was rasping loudly in the background. My friend hummed an accompanying note, slid to a second note, then added some chantlike syllables, and before long he was singing an exotic duet with the espresso machine. So exquisitely beautiful was this music that it affected me profoundly. From the moment it began, I was filled with the joy of the Holy Spirit—a joy that lingered long afterward and that returns even now as I recall this jocund noise. Excitedly I encouraged my friend to record his own CD of duets with trucks, razors, mixers, perhaps even leaf blowers. That day I came home with a new respect, even a newfound tenderness, toward machines.

My usual dislike of machines is called prejudice, an attitude one can hold toward anything—people, work, weather, politics. A joyful person, however, cannot afford to harbor prejudice. Joy is happy only when the whole world lies open before it, untrammeled and uncensored. The real world is a much larger and more wonderful place than the small corner of it we tend to inhabit. At times this larger world unexpectedly opens wide, and the way of joy is to swallow prejudice, walk deliberately toward the unlovely, and discover the song in it.

SIMPLE PLEASURES

With joy you will draw water from the wells of salvation.

ISAIAH 12:3

I'm a longtime fan of jazz pianist Keith Jarrett. During my experiment I ordered a copy of his latest CD titled *The Melody at Night, with You.* It happened to arrive on a day when I was feeling low, but as I listened to the first cut, I felt extraordinarily infused with quiet joy. Here, I thought, was something exquisitely beautiful because of its sheer artlessness and simplicity. Here was the sound of pure soul.

It helps to know something of Keith Jarrett's story. A prodigious performer, in 1996 he fell victim to chronic fatigue and had to give up public concerts. *The Melody at Night* was his first CD since then. Here's his own account of how it came about:

I started taping it in December of 1997, as a Christmas present for my wife. I'd just had my Hamburg Steinway overhauled and wanted to try it out, and I have my studio right next to the house, so if I woke up and had a half-decent day, I would turn on the tape recorder and play for a few minutes. I was too fatigued to do more. Then something started to click with the mike placement, the new action of the instrument—I could play *so soft*—and the internal dynamics of the melodies of the songs. It was one of those little miracles that you have to be ready for, though part of it was that I just didn't have the energy to be clever.... So the album ended up being about how you play melody without cleverness.[19]

That last phrase—"how you play melody without cleverness"—isn't that an apt description of the inner workings of joy? Again and again in this book I've had to fight the urge to be too clever, for joy doesn't lie in that direction. Joy is a simple pleasure that will not be courted by the intellect. As with all soul music, one cannot figure out joy, one can only feel it out.

In my experiment I was committed to uncovering the deep wells of joy in my life. Such wells are not always readily identified. One must search for them as for rare wildlife in a jungle. Unless we define for ourselves the specific, personal ways we experience joy and deliberately make room for these pleasures, happiness will escape us.

Sitting alone in my darkened living room with Keith Jarrett, I experienced a simple pleasure that I hadn't much indulged for years—listening to music, especially piano music, and not doing anything else; not using music as background, but letting the sound alone completely enfold my attention. Realizing how deeply I missed this pleasure, ever since that day I've cultivated it. For me it's a remarkably reliable source of joy.

To recover joy, it may be necessary to treat her like a casual acquaintance with whom one wishes to become good friends. She truly is like a person, having her peculiar character and tastes. If we don't know her well, isn't it because we've spurned her company, crowding our days with lesser companions? How might we go about befriending joy? Like anyone, she wants to be noticed, appreciated, cherished, enjoyed. Listen to the words of the old Shaker hymn "Simple Gifts":

'Tis the gift to be simple, 'tis the gift to be free,
'Tis the gift to come down where we ought to be;
And when we find ourselves in the place just right,
'Twill be in the valley of love and delight.

CLOSER THAN YOU THINK

There is a time for everything:…
a time to weep and a time to laugh,
a time to mourn and a time to dance.

ECCLESIASTES 3:1,4

Let's be frank. Despite all the Bible's exhortations to rejoice in the Lord, Ecclesiastes is right: We aren't going to be happy all the time. There are occasions when it's most appropriate to weep and mourn. Joy, after all, is just one aspect of the Holy Spirit's fruit, and sometimes it's important to emphasize others such as patience or self-control. At such times, joy may seem to have fled—but has it really? No, if the Holy Spirit is present, so is joy.

Communion with God is something like the weather: There are sunny days, overcast days, storms. But the sky never goes away. While varying conditions will affect our reception of the Spirit, joy depends upon making the most of whatever light there is, even in darkness. If you're in the season of winter, why not at least light a fire on the hearth? If you're having the sort of day that rates a two out of ten, why not make it the best two possible? I can testify from experience that the top end of two feels a lot better than the bottom end. In reaching for the top of two, I've often been surprised to find my hand closing around ten. Joy is always closer than we think.

Sometimes it's necessary to pass through sadness, even depression, in order to access happier feelings. Heartache can be a good teacher, and God can be glorified through us in spite of our mood. However, there's a difference between honest mourning and self-pity, between healthy sadness and denial.

Jesus wept for Lazarus, and a few moments later He raised him from the dead. Happy people aren't happy all the time, but they're never sad for long. They're always in motion, moving toward joy.

As long as some people seem happy by nature, without having to work much at it, we must admit that happiness isn't necessarily a sign of great faith or maturity, but a gift of grace. Does God, then, sometimes withhold the gift? No, happiness is God's great desire for us and He's made every provision for our joy. The Christian life is never one of hopeless misery; the world's unhappiness is not God's doing but ours. This is not to say the unhappy person should feel guilty, for guilt will only prolong and exacerbate unhappiness. Rather it means that every day, every moment, provides possibilities for joy. In no situation is it impossible to turn to the light. Just as "when you are tempted, he will also provide a way out" (1 Corinthians 10:13), so God always points a way out of woe.

Admittedly, happiness is contingent upon many factors that may be beyond our control. We're not individuals merely, but part of a family, a church, a community, a culture, a world, a spiritual realm. In the latter sphere alone, who knows what events may transpire daily, even hourly, to send ripples or shock waves through the tranquil pool of our personal joy?

This doesn't mean that we're helpless or that we have no influence over the course of joy. No one has a greater impact on our joy than we do. While all the factors affecting joy are not within our reach, it's helpful to act as if they are. Until we start reaching for joy in all circumstances, we'll have no idea how happy we can be. Much more of our happiness rests with us than we tend to believe. Taking full responsibility for our emotional state is itself a powerful step toward joy.

With all of life's various moods and seasons, a happy day may not always be attainable. But a happy life is. By acting as if happiness is always within our grasp, we put ourselves in the best position to live happily. Only the impossible is worth the effort.

A FIRM FOUNDATION

Let us fix our eyes on Jesus,
the author and perfecter of our faith,
who for the joy set before him endured the cross.

HEBREWS 12:2

The moment we imagine being happy all the time, a thousand objections present themselves.

"But I'm a naturally moody person. I've always been this way."

"I have an artistic temperament. To be creative, I need my lows as well as my highs."

"Isn't it normal to pass through different seasons in life?"

Many people will not commit themselves to happiness because they view it as too narrow, perhaps even selfish, a goal. Life is richer and more complex than that, they reason; they don't want to stick their heads in the sand. Much that is vital and necessary does not involve joy. Look at Jesus: When He went to the cross He wasn't pursuing personal happiness, was He? He had something larger in mind. The Declaration of Independence asserts the right to the pursuit of happiness, but does the gospel?

Hebrews 12:2 states plainly the reason Jesus went to the cross: joy. He didn't sacrifice His own happiness for the sake of some larger goal. Rather, looking through the darkness to the light beyond, He was animated by the prize of joy, knowing that pursuing this would release joy to others.

An unhappy person cannot make anyone else happy. The only way to bless others is to be joyful oneself. Seekers of joy need have no worries about becoming narrow-minded; rest assured that life's roughness and pain will seek you out, whether you're open to it or not. As for joy, however, if you don't search for it with all your heart, and commit yourself to doing whatever's necessary to attain it, you'll miss out. No one escapes suffering, but many lives are devoid of joy.

If we picture happiness as shallow, probably we harbor the same misconception about heaven. "God is a drag and heaven will be a big bore. The joy the Bible talks about is solemn, not something you can really have fun with. Certainly nothing you'd want to experience forever." Let's face it: The reason we don't trust happiness is the same reason we don't trust God. We don't want to box ourselves in; we want to be broad-minded and leave our options open. Yet paradoxically, "Small is the gate and narrow the road that leads to life, and only a few find it" (Matthew 7:14).

To be happy is not to be cut off from the full gamut of normal feelings. Happy people do not lobotomize their minds or castrate their emotions. Indeed they experience all their feelings more deeply than others. Moodiness is the deadening of healthy emotion, whereas joy is emotionally alive. Anyone who doesn't allow room for sadness, anger, and suffering cannot remain happy. The joy of the Lord is all-inclusive, deriving its strength from the very fact that it has carefully considered every aspect of reality under the sun, yet still remains happy.

Choose to build your life on anything but joy, and you'll be unstable. Only joy provides a foundation firm enough to support the entire life of the soul. God's name "I AM" (Exodus 3:14) denotes His constancy—the same yesterday, today, and tomorrow. We, by contrast, are characterized by inconstancy—so much so that we can hardly conceive of being joyful all the time. We sidestep the challenge of such a life by calling it too narrow, when really we're evading the development of a character as dependable as God's.

HOLD ON

The seed is the word of God.... Those on the rock
are the ones who receive the word with joy when they hear it,
but they have no root. They believe for a while,
but in the time of testing they fall away.

LUKE 8:11,13

I n Jesus' parable of the sower, the seed of God's Word is received with joy even by those with stony hearts, yet they're unable to retain it. While this story is about different kinds of people, it's also about different conditions of the human heart. The same heart can be stony or thorny one day, receptive and fertile another day.

What's the condition of your heart today? Have you received the Word of God joyfully? Or have you let His joy slip through your fingers? Maybe you refused joy when He offered it, preferring to nurse some grudge? Psalm 95:7-8 warns, "Today, if you hear his voice, do not harden your hearts." The author of Hebrews, quoting this verse, exhorts us to "encourage one another daily, as long as it is called Today" (3:13). What day is it? If the answer is today, then it's a day for joy.

If you feel that God has not spoken to you joyfully today, what about yesterday? Or did God perhaps give you joy last week, and this week you've forgotten it? Is your root shallow, or do you retain well the joy of the Lord? If you've ever been joyful in the past, why did you let go of it? Is the good news any less good today than when you first heard it? Has it become stale news for you? If it was good enough to set you free in the first place, isn't it good enough to set you free from your present crisis? Therefore, "Just as you received Christ Jesus as Lord, continue to live in him" (Colossians 2:6).

Joy is one of the ways the Lord confirms His Word to us. He may tell us to do something difficult, but because His direction comes with joy, we believe Him and are motivated to obey. If we forget the joy He gave, we'll lose the power to carry out His commands. Failing to recall joyful experiences, we lose hold of the promises attached to them. Jesus promises that "whoever drinks the water I give him will never thirst" (John 4:14). We need to develop a deep root, one that drinks enough water when it rains to last through a dry spell.

Remembering and retaining joy takes work, which is why the New Testament continually exhorts us to "hold on to the good" (1 Thessalonians 5:21). People must hold on to something. If I don't hold the good, then I'll hold the bad and stay stuck in problems. My experiment taught me to feel differently about problems. Where before I'd experienced them as maddeningly engrossing, now they became like old flames with whom I long ago fell out of love. They didn't have the power to entice me as before. In the light of my happy marriage to joy, it was easier to throw them off. Chronic problems have a way of going round and round on a hamster wheel, and a joyful person loses interest in this. Joy has better things to do.

Trouble will come, make no mistake. At times the joyful life looks like lashing myself to the mast in a storm. Yes, I'll be tested to the limits of endurance, for if I'm not, how will I ever know the limitlessness of joy? The more I hold to the good in such times, the stronger grows my grip. It's as if a hole, or many holes, have been plugged in my spirit, making me no longer a sieve but rather a vessel capable of containing all the fullness of the Holy Spirit.

PERSEVERANCE

Let us throw off everything that hinders
and the sin that so easily entangles,
and let us run with perseverance the race marked out for us.

HEBREWS 12:1

The word that catches my eye in this verse is *easily.* How easily we let the smallest difficulties erase our joy! The lawn mower breaks down, our nose stuffs up, a yowling cat disturbs our sleep, and suddenly our lot in life appears cruel and unfair. If we lose our cool over such minor annoyances, how will we face real tragedy?

As it turns out, the amount of joy in our lives doesn't hinge upon the weight of our suffering. There's actually no relation between these two factors. Some people who have suffered great tragedy possess great joy, while others who have never experienced tragedy never experience joy either. Perhaps the real tragedy is not all the bad that can befall us, but our tendency to live joylessly no matter how good we have it.

When I hear people complain that they cannot be happy because of this or that terrible event, I want to ask: Were you happy before the terrible event? Were you a joyful person in normal circumstances, and then tragedy stole your joy? Or have you always been miserable? To be sure, some tragedies date back to early childhood, making it seem that life has never been, nor ever could be, "normal." But here too some people who apparently had healthy childhoods grow up to be miserable, while others emerge from childhood trauma to learn the secrets of joy.

No rules and laws cover such things. Instead there's only the mystery of each human heart freely running its individual course before God, opting at each step either for grumbling or gratitude, for woe or joy.

In this race sin easily entangles. It doesn't take much to get us off track. If marathon runners were as easily sidelined in their race as most of us are in the pursuit of happiness, few would ever complete the twenty-six mile course. Why do we exhibit greater perseverance in achieving worldly goals—winning medals, earning degrees, writing books—than in gaining the prize of joy? As a writer I know I can write this book; I've written books before. Why not also admit that I know how to be happy? I had a happy day yesterday; I can chalk up another one today. Like running a race, it's a matter of putting one foot in front of the other.

The author of Hebrews challenges us to "throw off everything that hinders" in running this race. The New Testament calls this quality "perseverance" and links it intimately with joy. As Paul puts it, we "rejoice in our sufferings, because we know that suffering produces perseverance" (Romans 5:3). Scripture doesn't separate joy and suffering; they're held together by perseverance. Nor does perseverance mean grimly gritting one's teeth; there's real joy in it. There's joy in discipline, joy in single-mindedness, joy in straightforwardly completing what one sets out to do. The key to such perseverance is wholehearted resolve. If only we'll resolve to do something with all our hearts, it's as good as done. Joy rests in our discovery of the unlimited power inherent in a thoroughgoing resolve—including the resolve to be happy at whatever cost.

A prison warden who had weathered many riots once told me his secret: "In the middle of a crisis, I plan for the resolution. In a week or a month I know this thing will blow over, so I start planning for that time now." Perseverance is planning for the resolution. Chronic miseries are produced by fear; miracles come through faith.

JESUS' SECRET

We rejoice in the hope of the glory of God.
Not only so, but we also rejoice in our sufferings.

ROMANS 5:2-3

When C. S. Lewis titled his early autobiography *Surprised by Joy,* he little realized how strangely prophetic this phrase would be. Late in life the author was literally surprised by a woman named Joy whom he married and who shortly afterward died of cancer. For Lewis, as for every authentic Christian, joy and suffering came profoundly, inextricably mixed.

In the New Testament, joy and suffering are so entwined that we're continually exhorted to "rejoice in our sufferings." The same apostle who wrote "Rejoice in the Lord always" described himself as "sorrowful, yet always rejoicing" and stated plainly, "In all our troubles my joy knows no bounds" (2 Corinthians 6:10; 7:4). In Romans he testified to being "full of joy" and also to having "great sorrow and unceasing anguish in my heart" (16:19; 9:2). How can this be?

To be joyful is to know how to handle suffering, how to marry it with joy. As we suffer well, threads of joy interweave our pain, like fingers clasped so closely in prayer that one hand cannot be distinguished from the other. Consider Jesus' promise, "My yoke is easy and my burden is light" (Matthew 11:30). No one has ever felt more the weight of the world and its anguish than Jesus, yet He spoke of a burden that is light, not heavy. What was His secret?

Jesus' secret is the cross. The cross is the collision between reality and religious expectation. The cross is all that part of life that cannot seem to be spiritualized, that refuses to be enveloped by a nice, warm glow. The cross is everything we don't want life to be like, but it is. Jesus bids us take up this cross, for as we do, we'll find it light. If the cross we're carrying is heavy, we may have picked up the wrong one. Let's put down the heavy cross and find the cross that is light. Jesus doesn't want us shouldering heavy weights. He shoulders the load for us. Yes, we're destined to share Christ's suffering, yet none of us can suffer as He did, for "the punishment that brought us peace was upon him, and by his wounds we are healed" (Isaiah 53:5).

The joy of the Lord draws the fangs of suffering. The world despises suffering, but joy finds in these broken places a happy home. No situation is so bleak that it cannot be reached by joy. If at times all you can do is suffer, do it well. You can still pray to be set free, but prayer means asking and trusting, not pouting and demanding. More joy comes from trust than from a sense of self-mastery.

How is the cross coming to you right now? Disease? Divorce? The death of a loved one? There's only one thing to do with this cross: Pick it up and rejoice. We'll recognize the cross of Christ because, as we pick it up, it feels light. The cross is heavy only when we shoulder it unwillingly. Our own bitterness weighs it down.

Jesus' cross is the union of joy and suffering. Our sinful nature believes that in order to be joyful we must get rid of suffering, but this is a lie. The truth is that joy exists precisely in the acceptance of the suffering we strive so strenuously to avoid. Prisoners arriving at this realization have been known to kiss their fetters.

RAISE THE ROOF

Everyone who has will be given more,
and he will have an abundance. Whoever does not have,
even what he has will be taken from him.

MATTHEW 25:29

To be happy is to count oneself among the haves, not the have-nots. Joy comes from having all we need and more. When we have an abundance, we're thankful, and thankfulness feeds joy so that we have more and more. Though we sit down to an empty table, we give thanks and somehow the food of joy arrives, just as happened when Jesus fed a multitude with one boy's lunch. Being thankful for what we have, however little it may seem, means we never want for happiness.

When we see ourselves as have-nots, on the other hand, the thieves of discontent and anxiety quickly set to work, stealing even what we have. This is what happened to Adam and Eve, as the serpent provoked in them a sense of have-not, and they lost Paradise. People were created to be happy, and there's no reason not to be. Unhappiness is understandable but not defensible. When we're fooled into being unhappy, unhappiness itself becomes our downfall. All sin stems from discontent, whereas the person who is joyful in the Lord will not go astray.

Adam and Eve need not have been greedy. If only they'd been happy with Paradise, they would have been given more and more, because happiness is inherently cumulative. Joy in the Lord is a living thing, eternally alive, ever growing. Nothing can stop it from penetrating deeper and deeper into the kingdom of heaven, to which there is no end.

Looking back over my Christian life, I see how my faith in God has grown steadily, at times almost measurably from day to day. Even in dark times I've sensed intuitively that my faith was still growing. Why shouldn't the same be true of joy? Why shouldn't joy be like a tree, a giant sequoia, that just grows and grows? A tree never bumps its head on the sky; why should joy? Joy has no ceiling.

When the disciples were faced with the resurrected Jesus, "they still did not believe it because of joy and amazement" (Luke 24:41). Like them, we cannot seem to believe that joy is real and will last. No doubt we've often been disappointed, yet our very disappointment drives joy away. Our very fear that joy cannot last ensures that it cannot, for we've labeled it not as something we have but as something we have not. It's not yet ours. To make it ours we must leave the company of the have-nots and join the haves, those who know that the joy they now have will grow and grow so that they'll always have an abundance.

Imagine a magician reaching into his hat to pull out what the audience supposes to be a short length—maybe ten feet—of red ribbon. Meanwhile the magician knows that he has secretly stashed a hundred yards of ribbon in the hat. So he starts to pull, and he pulls and pulls, and after about fifty feet the audience is gasping. Where's it all coming from?

Now imagine that the ribbon doesn't stop after a hundred yards. To the magician's own surprise, it keeps coming and coming—two hundred yards, three hundred, five hundred…a mile! By this point the magician is on his knees, shouting in jubilant amazement. This truly is magic! More than magic, it's miracle. To this hat there's no bottom, and this is how it is with the joy of the Lord.

A PERMANENT CHANGE

Your grief will turn to joy....
No one will take away your joy....
Your joy will be complete.

JOHN 16:20-24

Five times in these five verses Jesus promises joy. I'm particularly struck by His words, "No one will take away your joy." Obviously He's talking about something permanent.

When I began to be consistently happy, at first I was fearful lest my happiness soon fade away, just as it always had. Joy, I believed, could not possibly be permanent. Or could it? If it's true that nothing can "separate us from the love of God that is in Christ Jesus" (Romans 8:39), might not the same be true of joy in the Lord?

My experiment included humdrum days, days when I cannot honestly say I felt much joy. Maybe I'd slept badly, and the morning would begin with a troubling phone call, then I'd face a mountain of laundry, errands to run, a meeting to attend, and in the midst of a tight schedule something would go wrong, and for various reasons I'd be kept on the go all day long with barely a chance to catch my breath. Though such a day held little real joy, finding that I could live it without grumbling was new for me. So satisfying was this newfound equanimity that, reflecting on it at the end of the day, I'd feel deep joy return, just as if it had been there all along, waiting for me to notice.

Indeed, joy *was* there all along, because joy is not a thing but a capacity of the heart. If you put an addition on your house, the house is bigger. This change is permanent; the house never returns to its old size. Similarly whenever joy increases, a permanent change takes place. All at once you know joy as something bigger than you ever realized. A new capacity for joy has been created in the heart, and the heart remembers this. Joy itself remembers the size and shape and feel of its home within you.

Joy is a part of you. You *are* joy. You and I are the Lord's joy, and He is ours, and we are each other's. Paul calls the Philippians "my joy and crown" (4:1); the psalmist calls God "my joy and my delight" (43:4); God calls His "people a joy" (Isaiah 65:18). Since joy is not a possession but something we are, we cannot lose it.

In practice this means that if ever I do feel cut off from joy, it's no more serious than misplacing my car keys. Indeed it's less serious, for in the case of joy the loss is an illusion. I can lose my keys, but I cannot really lose joy. After all, where would it go? Would the joy of the Lord fall out of my pocket and drop into some black hole? No, joy is a permanent facet of the character of God who lives in me by His Holy Spirit. The more I believe this, the more it changes me, and the more this change is no flash in the pan but a permanent change of character.

Jesus gives His word that my joy will never be taken away. It inhabits a place in me that nothing and no one else can touch or influence, so long as I'm careful to honor that place. I may surrender my joy, but no person, nor any circumstance, can take it from me. It's here to stay so long as I trust it. When I keep a wary eye on joy, fearful that she'll slip away, I cannot fully relax to enjoy her. To the extent that I disbelieve in joy's permanence, I'll find her to be a fickle friend—exactly as fickle as my faith.

MAKING IT LAST

On that day they offered great sacrifices,
rejoicing because God had given them great joy.

NEHEMIAH 12:43

When the Lord gives great joy, do you use it for rejoicing in Him, or do you put it to more practical use? Often I catch myself putting joy to work—using it to get more writing done, to make endless plans, to run all kinds of errands. Being joyful is like having a fat wad of money to go shopping with, and my brain and body move faster and faster as I race from store to store. By the end of my frantic spending spree, I wonder what has happened to all my joy. Are the things I've exchanged for joy really worth the cost?

While there's nothing wrong with making practical use of joy's energy, getting things done isn't the primary purpose of joy. Joy's purpose is to rejoice in God, the Joy Giver, and in all His good works. As this remains our focus, our joy will last.

Yes, joy is of great practical value, yet it can also easily deteriorate into frivolity and be frittered away on nothing. When we're happy, we feel good, not just emotionally but morally, and this can be a dangerous combination. We may start to think more highly of ourselves than we ought, and then a surprisingly small event can trigger a powerful mood change. Sometimes the greater the joy, the more volatile it is. A buoyant person is just as liable to fall into temptation as a sad one, but the buoyant person has farther to fall.

Often we lose joy because we don't know how to hold on to it. We need to learn to relish joy without dissipation. The word *dissipation* refers to a wasting or squandering, an indulgence in pleasure to the point of harming oneself.

Many Christians who are temperate in regard to smoking or alcohol are intemperate in the use of joy. Gladly we milk a slaphappy mood for all it's worth, then wonder why we crash and end up with an emotional hangover. To sustain joy we must be just as self-controlled in happy times as we are self-searching in sorrowful times.

Prior to his conversion, C. S. Lewis spent years in an increasingly frustrated pursuit of what he called "Joy." Finally he concluded he was "wrong in supposing that I desired Joy itself. Joy itself, considered simply as an event in my own mind, turned out to be of no value at all. All the value lay in that of which Joy was the desiring." Lewis wanted not merely joy, but the "something other, outside" to which joy pointed.[20]

Worldly people may be happy for any number of reasons, but Christian joy is joy in the Lord. Godly rejoicing is a pure and selfless activity of soul with no ulterior motive. As joy is freely given, so it is freely returned to its Source with no strings attached. Subordinate activities may accompany rejoicing, but if the rejoicing itself is not pure to the point of sacrifice, joy will soon dissipate.

Those who are joyful make great sacrifices, whereas the unhappy have little to give. The joyful have unlimited resources because they're plugged into the Source of joy and of every other good thing. Knowing their joy is not self-produced but is given by God, and confident also that God is unstinting in His giving, they know there's no end to their joy. The pure act of rejoicing in God perpetually renews their joy.

It would be foolish to invest a lot of energy in pursuing happiness but none in learning to retain it. Believing happiness to be fickle by nature, we tend to behave in a reckless, fickle manner toward it. If only we would be faithful to joy, it would be faithful to us, for it's a manifestation of God's own unchanging character.

LIVING IN MYSTERY

Splendor and majesty are before him;
strength and joy in his dwelling place.

1 CHRONICLES 16:27

We all have questions for God. Don't we also know, secretly and sheepishly, that if somehow we could be with God right now, our questions would melt away? Just to be with Him would be answer enough.

Well, guess what? We *are* with Him, and He's with us. Why not relax and enjoy Him? While unanswered questions can be frustrating, they can also be a powerful source of joy. Do you gnaw anxiously at questions, or do you see them as intriguingly wrapped gifts that, at the appropriate time, will reveal their contents? Have you room for mystery in your life?

Joy itself is a mystery. Sometimes I have it and I don't know why. Other times searching for it is like trying to find the mouth of a cave underwater. Why is joy by turns so mysteriously available and so maddeningly elusive?

The reason is that joy is a divine Person who does as He pleases. Joy will not dance to our tune; we must dance to His. And we do. Often our happiness is not the result of anything we've done or even anything we believe, but rather it's the Lord Himself rejoicing over some secret known to Him alone. To live in joy, it isn't necessary to figure out this secret or to have all the answers to our problems. When the Person who does have the answers is present, suddenly the questions lose their urgency, for our deepest longing is not for answers but for Him. Ultimately we're happier and more satisfied with mysteries than with any amount of explanation.

Joy is rooted not in what, when, why, or how, but in who. Meanings and explanations can get in the way of experiencing the greatest joy of all, which is simply to be with the Divine Lover without any other meaning except being together. If we understood all mysteries, our joy could not be as great, for joy feeds upon a God of splendor and majesty who is far beyond our comprehension.

Perhaps we're living on the outskirts of God's kingdom, deliberately avoiding all we don't understand. How would it feel to move downtown where the action is? Without a love for the incomprehensible, how can we love ourselves? If we're uncomfortable with the unknown, how can we relax enough to act spontaneously? Nothing surprising will happen to us because we'll never do anything out of character. Though our lives be founded on good Christian principles backed up with plenty of Bible verses, we may never experience real joy. The Bible is full of passages we've never noticed because we've never taken an unknown path—never had coffee with a drug addict, never water-skied or parasailed, never invited all our friends to one big party, never danced in the rain with the one we love.

There are times when joy comes only from setting aside the black book (not the Bible itself, but our own narrow interpretation of it) and acting in total freedom—stepping outside the old boundaries and doing something we've never done before, something strange and wild and steeped in mystery. Then we'll know the joy not only of embracing the mystery that is, but of adding more mystery as we go. More and more we'll surprise ourselves by acting in ways so mysterious that they can be explained only as the Lord acting through us.

THE DIVINE GARDENER

The LORD has done great things for us,
and we are filled with joy.

PSALM 126:3

One evening, at a low point in my experiment, I was sitting in the audience at a school concert. I felt dull, restless, detached. All at once something happened that I cannot explain. It had nothing to do with events onstage. Rather, for some reason I found myself staring at a man in the audience a couple of rows ahead of me. Suddenly his head, of which I could see only the back, seemed to be my own head. Though he didn't look at all like me, I felt exactly as if I were looking at myself in a mirror. A most peculiar sensation.

Moreover I felt I could look inside this head and read the thoughts there. They were my own thoughts, yet seeing them at a distance, as if outside myself, they lost their immediacy and power. I'd been preoccupied with thoughts of unhappiness, wondering why I wasn't joyful and what to do about it. Now, with stunning clarity, I saw how my thinking was warped with anxious manipulation, with pitiful striving and conniving.

At that moment the Lord intervened to brush aside all these vain thoughts like so much mist. Then, taking a tiny grain of real joy on the tip of His finger, He thrust it deep into my heart, just like a gardener planting a seed.

Well! I came away from that concert singing with lighthearted abandon, and that night I slept like a baby. The following day I was filled with such great joy and energy that I hardly knew what to do with it all. The Lord God had planted in me one small seed of joy that for days afterward bore a rich harvest, putting to shame all the futile schemes of my overheated human brain. Once again God had demonstrated that heavenly joy does not come from earthly plans, but rather "every good and perfect gift is from above, coming down from the Father of the heavenly lights" (James 1:17).

This doesn't mean we make no effort to plan for happiness and work toward it. Rather, it means joy is too pure and holy, too fathomless and uncreated, to be of any human origin. What good, then, is all our work? Perhaps its chief value is to give us some small awareness of the cost of joy on God's part. Joy will never come to the lazy fatalist because such a person cannot appreciate its worth.

In the final stages of my experiment, I felt my joy significantly deepen, as more and more it seemed to proceed directly from God rather than from anything I did. Even as my joy increased, however, my weariness with the experiment also increased, until I had the amazing sense of God carrying me, sustaining me in surprisingly effortless joy. Yes, I know He wants me to keep on working, fighting, believing, obeying—yet He also wants me to know that joy is His free gift and that He can produce it in me (or do anything else in or through me) all by Himself, without my help at all.

Have you discovered yet that the Christian life is impossible? In the words of Norman Grubb, "You can't live the Christian life;" rather, "Christ is in you and He will live the life."[21] If you're skeptical of being happy every day, it's because you believe it's impossible. It is. This is exactly the point. We cannot achieve the life of God on our own. We can no more create joy in ourselves than we can pull real rabbits out of hats. Joy is God's work; faith is ours.

EVERLASTING JOY

Everlasting joy will crown their heads.
Gladness and joy will overtake them,
and sorrow and sighing will flee away.

ISAIAH 51:11

At times while writing this book, I worried about running out of ideas. How much is it possible to say on this one rather narrow topic of joy? Then, when I least expected it, God would surprise me with fresh joy and a burst of new thoughts. Gradually I realized that I would never run out of joyous inspiration, because I'm connected to the Source of Joy whose thoughts are unlimited. Indeed it's in the nature of joy to know there's no end to what it enjoys. Joy doesn't feed on the transitory but on the eternal.

We don't have to wait until after we die to experience everlasting joy. If it's everlasting, it exists now and always has. Joy is like a river that has always been flowing; all we need do is step into the flow.

Some days when I'm sad I'll look out at the trees, the flowers, the sky—all these wonders that at times have brought me so much joy—and I'll think, *Why don't I feel it now? What's wrong?* All that's wrong is that I'm listening to lies. Nothing essential in this beautiful scene has changed, but a voice in my head drones, "The beauty in these things is all used up. It's gone and you won't feel it again." Or sometimes the voice whispers, "The beauty is right there, but you can't reach it. Maybe tomorrow, but not today. Today is spoiled; you've messed it up beyond recovery. Don't you remember you've been banished from the Garden?"

These are lies. The beauty of God's creation is eternal (though the creation itself passes away), and listening to this lying voice is the reason we were banished in the first place. How long will we keep entertaining "the father of lies" (John 8:44)?

The further I progressed in my experiment, the more I discovered unhappiness to be illusory. It would descend upon me unawares, creeping into my thoughts like a sinister fog, so that for a while I might not notice what was happening. As soon as I did notice, I became increasingly skilled at shrugging off the fog of lies and basking in the happy truth. Today I'm amazed at how easily this can be done. Gloomy moods that formerly held me for hours or days can now be shaken off in a moment, just by recognizing their source and their ephemerality.

For unbelievers, unhappiness is real; it will last forever. But for believers unhappiness is unreal because it passes away. About every woe we can say with confidence, "This too will pass." Perfect joy will be ours forever in heaven, showing our current struggles to be fleeting shadows by comparison. Though earthly joys are also mere shadows compared with the joys to come, still we're called to start building the kingdom of heaven here and now. It's no use complaining we're imperfect, because the fact that God's "power is made perfect in weakness" (2 Corinthians 12:9) creates unlimited possibilities for being filled this side of heaven with "the whole measure of the fullness of Christ" (Ephesians 4:13). Since our destination is sure, we can rejoice now just as if we're already there.

Joy is like a beautiful place that, once seen, can never be forgotten. At times we seem to have strayed from this place, and we wonder how to get back. Eventually, however, we realize that this place is not out *there* somewhere but *here,* inside us, a permanent place in our heart. The clearer our grasp of this truth, the more we may taste of everlasting joy now.

RESURRECTION

Brothers, we do not want you to be ignorant
about those who fall asleep, or to grieve
like the rest of men, who have no hope.

1 THESSALONIANS 4:13

The happiest person I've ever seen was lying in a coffin.

Here's what happened: In November 1996 I was away from home at a conference. It was Sunday morning, and I had a hotel room with a balcony overlooking beautiful Harrison Lake in British Columbia. When I awoke about eight o'clock, I felt filled with an extraordinary, otherworldly joy. It was the deepest, purest joy I'd ever felt. At the time I couldn't figure it out; it bore no apparent connection to any event. For a long time I lay in bed basking in ecstasy, and later I sat on the balcony to gaze in rapture at the tranquillity of the lake and the distant mountains. Throughout that day this unusual joy lingered and clung to me.

Late that evening I returned home and went to bed around midnight. At six o'clock the phone rang, and my father, his voice cracking, told me that my mother had passed away the previous morning. Her death had occurred at the very moment I awoke in the hotel room. Suddenly the mystery of the wonderful joy that had visited me was solved, and through this outpouring of bliss I knew beyond a shadow of doubt that my mother had gone straight to heaven to be with Jesus forever.

I needed to know this. My mother never discussed matters of faith with me; I had scant idea what she believed. Without the evidence of joy I would have been left in the dark as to her eternal destiny.

Joy comprehends secrets that cannot be known in any other way. Joy is prophetic, the firstfruits of the profound and everlasting happiness toward which all the faithful are progressing more rapidly than we think. This is the only possible comfort in the face of death. Joy is a message from the heart of God that all is well.

Not only is joy prophetic, it's pragmatic. After talking with my father on the phone I immediately made flight arrangements, packed my bags, and embarked on a long day of travel. Throughout the ensuing week, crammed with countless duties and details, joy was my constant companion. Truly I experienced the truth of Nehemiah 8:10—"Do not grieve, for the joy of the LORD is your strength." This isn't to say I felt no grief, for I certainly did. But I did not "grieve like the rest of men, who have no hope," for I had solid evidence that my mother is in the happiest place imaginable, where I'll soon see her again.

There's more to this story. At the funeral home the family members gathered around the open casket for a short prayer led by the minister. Uncharacteristically, during the prayer I kept my eyes open and looked steadily at my mother's face. I knew these few moments were my last chance on earth to look upon her physical form, and I wanted to remember her clearly. In the past few years her health had been poor and she suffered much, but now she appeared ten years younger, relaxed and mysteriously natural. The moment the prayer began, it seemed to me some color came into her face, a touch of life and warmth, and throughout the prayer the vividness of this impression grew and grew until I actually felt that Mom was smiling. By the close of the prayer her whole face was alight and she looked radiantly peaceful and joyful. As soon as the amen was said, this impression faded, and a few moments later the casket was closed for the last time. But I had a memory that would last forever—an indelible mental photograph of my mother bathed in glory, the happiest face I've ever seen.[22]

8 8

CONFIDENCE

Satisfy us in the morning with your unfailing love,
that we may sing for joy and be glad all our days.

PSALM 90:14

The author of Psalm 90 did not deem it an unreasonable goal to be full
of joy all his days—every day, all day long, for the rest of his life. However, he recognized that the prerequisite for this condition was to be satisfied
with God's unfailing love.

Knowing we're loved by God is the basis of joy. When I asked the most
joyful woman I know to tell me her secret, she replied unhesitatingly with one
word: "Confidence." My entire ninety-day experiment could be summed up
by this word, for I could not have begun without a good measure of confidence, and in confidence I ended. In retrospect, however, I see that the confidence I set out with was largely self-confidence, while in the end I arrived at
a much deeper confidence in the Lord. Between these two poles lies a world
of difference. The former, rooted in excitement, is brashly triumphalistic,
whereas the latter, rooted in amazement, is quietly adoring.

The quality of our lives depends upon the questions we ask. At the beginning of my experiment I faced each day with the question, "Will I be happy
today?" By the end I was asking, "What form will my happiness take?" The
reframing of this question radically changes how I live. Asking the question in
its first form, I live in anxiety. Putting it the second way, I live in confident
expectation.

A life of joy depends upon approaching each day not in fear or worry but
in the confidence of faith. The time when confidence is most needed is when
worldly circumstances most threaten it. "So do not throw away your confidence;

it will be richly rewarded" (Hebrews 10:35). Often we think of faith as something we must do, yet that's exactly what faith is not. Faith motivates us to work, but faith itself is concerned not at all with our work but only with God's work in us. Faith looks entirely to Him. "Blessed is the man who trusts in the LORD, whose confidence is in him" (Jeremiah 17:7). Joy springs from a deep, settled confidence that God's life in us is incorruptible and inalienable. We could hardly get rid of it if we tried. It's something God has done and His work is permanent.

Isn't this just where our faith is weakest? Rather than believing joy to be dependable, we see it as inherently capricious, and so we remain like corks tossed on a sea of wayward feelings. Does God really want us to be happy? Is joy really appropriate in this dark world? Is it practical or even possible to be joyful every day? As long as such questions remain, we cannot relax enough to be fully happy. Happiness depends upon answering these questions with a resounding *yes!* David felt such confidence when he ended Psalm 23, "Surely goodness and love will follow me all the days of my life."

By the end of ninety days my whole focus had shifted from myself—"Can I really do this?"—to God: "How wonderful He is to do this for me!" While in the beginning it seemed there was so much I had to do to maintain joy, in the end I felt that God was doing everything—steadying my nerves, clearing away my doubts, delivering me from trials, filling me with nearly continuous joy, and bringing me a new clarity about the accessibility of a joy-filled life for every believer. It was as if the Lord, the true Author of my faith, was at the last gathering up all the threads of my experiment and drawing them together toward a rich conclusion, much as a novelist brings his story to a happy ending.

ALL I SEE

How happy your men must be!
How happy your officials,
who continually stand before you
and hear your wisdom!

1 KINGS 10:8

T he words above are those of the Queen of Sheba upon visiting King
Solomon and experiencing his wisdom and the splendor of his court.
The queen correctly understood that true wisdom brings happiness and
spreads joy to all around.

How true is this of our churches? Are they places where wisdom reigns so
gloriously that the people are filled with happiness and visitors are overawed?
Solomon, despite all his wisdom, was seriously flawed, and his kingdom fell
into decline. As Christians, however, we have continual access to the court of
the King of kings in a kingdom "that can never perish, spoil or fade" (1 Peter
1:4). Unlike the Queen of Sheba, we don't have to travel many miles to a for-
eign capital to sit at the feet of wisdom, for the one true God, the majestic
Lord of heaven and earth, dwells within us by His Holy Spirit. Because "we
have the mind of Christ" (1 Corinthians 2:16), God speaks to us through our
very own thoughts. How happy we should be!

There's a story about a young boy who happened upon an artist painting
beside a small lake. Too shy to approach, the boy hid in the bushes to watch.
Every day for a week he returned, fascinated by the artist's paraphernalia of
brushes, paints, and easel, and especially by the subject matter of his pictures.
For all this time the artist painted only one thing—whales. Painting after

painting of whales. What, the boy wondered, was going on in this man's mind? There weren't any whales in a lake!

Eventually, as the boy's curiosity overcame his shyness, he approached the artist and began asking questions. When he could stand it no longer, finally he got around to asking the one big question that burned inside him.

"Tell me—why do you paint only whales?"

At this the artist looked off across the lake, a broad, misty smile lighting up his whole face, and he answered dreamily:

"I paint whales because they're all I see."[23]

As I near the end of writing this book, joy is all I see. Having examined and befriended it for so long now, truly it fills my vision. Though in this world I live, as it were, beside a small lake, perhaps even a pond, and haven't yet reached the dazzling ocean, nevertheless at heart I'm a seagoer. I sense the vastness of the deep and cannot resist its pull. By God's grace I'm there now, already at play in the ocean of joy. Whereas for years I kept wondering, spiritually speaking, where my next meal was coming from, now I find myself seated at the banquet table. While others go hungry, all I see is food. It's not that I don't also see and ache for the world's woe, but now from force of habit I cannot help but see past the woe to something more real, more permanent, more convincing, more spellbinding.

Novelist Michael O'Brien portrays a character who goes snow-blind while camping by a remote lake in northern Ontario. After lying in his tent for several weeks in midwinter, not only blind but in excruciating pain, the man regains his sight and runs outside to see what many people never see in their entire lives:

"It was too wonderful! I ran out and I saw!"

"What did you see?"

"I saw that everything is so beautiful we should fall down and worship God a hundred times a day."[24]

ECSTASY

Then the temple of the LORD was filled with a cloud,
and the priests could not perform their service because of the cloud,
for the glory of the LORD filled the temple of God.

2 CHRONICLES 5:13-14

Thinking and writing about joy day after day is like eating the food of angels. Often the diet seems too rich for my poor soul, and I must deliberately turn to some sober, mundane activity to stem the impassioned flow of my thoughts and anchor my feet to the ground. Every day God pours His joy into me, far more than I can possibly express in a book. It's as if He's been waiting for this, waiting for centuries, for eons, until the time when He could teach me, His son Michael, all about joy.

Oh, the secrets He reveals, the delights He lavishes on my soul! When two people love each other, they share things no one else in the world can know. Such deep secrets are incommunicable, sometimes even to oneself. They don't come to the soul adorned with any words, form, or rational content, but rather as a direct infusion of pure energy. Not only is it impossible to express such things, but one feels little inclination to do so, it being the private business of lovers.

What a pity! What books could be written if such mysteries could be told! As it is, in some ways I feel this book merely skims the surface of its subject, for whenever I approach the real depths and try to find words for the actual sensation of divine joy, something in me balks and I cannot quite do it. The very word *joy* is too weak and inadequate for such experience. The only word that comes close is *ecstasy.*

Ecstasy is supercharged joy communicated directly to the spirit with no discernible content. Ecstasy is so beyond rational thought that the best one can do is describe its external manifestation, how it typically occurs. For example, one morning during my experiment I awoke full of joy but without knowing why. I tried to write, but the joy was so strong that I soon lost all interest not only in writing but in doing anything at all. Though I tried to pray, I couldn't even do that. I couldn't think clearly, couldn't even place myself helplessly in God's presence. Finally I gave up and did absolutely nothing, at which point the joy escalated unimaginably, turning into pure euphoria with no focus, no substance, nothing to pin a single idea to. This was nothing but pure ecstasy itself, and in that state I lay for an hour or two, adrift on an ocean of rapture.

What is this? All I know is that it's God, God in such overwhelming purity that all one's circuits are blown. It's like a megadownload of far too much joyful information for anyone to process, let alone convey to others.

How ironic: I began my experiment thinking I could do certain things to cultivate joy. I wanted to investigate how to live, how to pray, how to walk with the Lord in joy every day and to communicate these principles to others. Yet ultimately I discovered that the deepest joy comes out of the blue, for no rhyme or reason, not because one is praying or meditating or feeling filled with faith, nor because one is being very good or has done anything right, but only because God Himself is all goodness and all rightness and because the depths of His joy surpass all understanding.

If the internal workings of ecstasy cannot be communicated, it's not because this experience is vague or obscure, but rather the opposite: As Mendelssohn said of the meaning of music, it's "too specific for words." Ecstasy is the last word on joy, the soul's champagne.

EPILOGUE

Come and share your master's happiness!

MATTHEW 25:21

In April 1994, five years before I began my experiment, I had a vision of Jesus. I was praying with a friend in my living room when suddenly Jesus stood before me. Though I call this a "vision," what happened was so utterly, fantastically real that it didn't seem like a vision. Purely and simply, I met Jesus of Nazareth face to face. There was no doubt in my mind that it really was He; I would have known Him anywhere.

I wasn't feeling particularly holy that day, indeed the opposite. A few hours later I'd be getting on a plane to join my parents for their fiftieth wedding anniversary, and I was preoccupied with plans for this event. I hadn't yet packed, I had a hundred details to attend to, and my mind was further distracted by my daughter's loud music in the next room. Hardly the setting for a quiet prayer time. When my friend suggested we pray, I agreed merely to humor him.

In this unlikely setting Jesus appeared to me. I've never had another vision, before or since, but this one so impacted me that I carry it with me always like a photo in the wallet of my heart. I see Him again now as I write, especially His face. If I were an artist I would paint Him. As it is, I'll say only that Jesus did not resemble any of the popular images I've seen. Rather, He was just as Isaiah described Him: "He had no beauty or majesty to attract us to him, nothing in his appearance that we should desire him" (53:2). Yes, the Jesus I saw is a decidedly unhandsome man. With any ordinary human, one might almost apply the word *ugly*—except Jesus is not ugly. He's beautiful. He's so radiant and loving that all normal standards of physical beauty are disqualified.

What mainly struck me was His joy. He was positively beaming with happiness, like ten thousand suns, and I felt that all this joy was directed at me. He was so glad to see me! Moreover He was inviting me to share His happiness.

I felt some response was called for—but what? I wanted to say something to my Lord, yet talking to the real, visible Jesus is quite different from saying prayers in an empty room. "Oh, Lord," I stammered, "it's so good to be with You…" Whatever I said came out sounding lame. Stupid, forced, artificial. Here I was with the chance of a lifetime and I was blowing it royally. Who did I think I was, seeing and talking to Jesus Christ?

At that point my vision faded. For a while I kept still, trying to bring Him back. But no, the experience was over. When eventually I opened my eyes I was back in the living room with my friend. The loud music was still playing and everything was the same as before. Yet everything was different because now I was filled with joy. I was ecstatic!

Somehow I got my bag packed and made it to the airport, and throughout the four-hour plane ride I leaned back in the chair and dreamed of Jesus, picturing His face again and again, studying Him from every angle. And after that I enjoyed the most wonderful visit I've ever had with my parents, celebrating their fifty years of marriage. I didn't tell anyone my experience; I didn't have to. I'd been filled with the joy of the Lord, and because of this all my contacts with people over the next few days took on a wholly different quality.

Nevertheless, while the joy of the vision stayed with me for several days, I couldn't live there. Normal life resumed, and eventually I found myself reflecting less on Jesus' happiness than on my own awkwardness. I felt badly because, face to face with the Lord, I hadn't known how to talk to Him, let alone how to share His joy. And so I was left with a sense of incompletion, which gradually modulated into an invitation.

This book, I believe, is the fulfillment of a commission Jesus gave me in that vision years ago. He was inviting me to share His happiness. At the time my faith was too halting, my self-doubt too strong even to imagine entering into a life of sustained joy. Yet an invitation from Jesus is a powerful summons, and now, by His grace, I have answered His call.

Through my experiment in joy, a whole new dimension of Christianity has opened up to me, like a beautiful flower blossoming from a bud long dormant. This new spirituality is of such sweetness, light, and grace that it entirely entrances me. I've always suspected the existence of this and have had many glimpses of it. What's different now is the confidence that I know the way into this new country and how to live there, because I've discovered for myself that it's real. I believe! Finally I believe enough in the Bible's offer of everlasting joy to see this great promise fulfilled in my own life. I shall never be the same. The veil of the world's lies has been torn away, and now I know for certain that the Christian life is meant to be entirely steeped in joy. With the author of Hebrews I can say that I've already come to "the city of the living God...to thousands upon thousands of angels in joyful assembly" (12:22).

My experiment has been wildly successful. Joy has indeed become an ingrained habit of my soul—so much a part of me that it hardly seems possible that I lived without it for nearly half a century. Not only am I much happier now than ever before, but I know it's possible to keep moving in the direction of joy and to have more and more of it. In the search for joy a certain point arrives where the balance tips in our favor. We find we're no longer striving for happiness; we're simply happy. It's like getting out of debt: Without a fat mortgage payment to dole out every month, life takes on an entirely different feel. Difficulties still come, perhaps grave ones, but joy keeps flowing into the hurts like a self-renewing stream.

Is it really possible to be happy all the time? Three years after my experiment, I still cannot quite join Brother Lawrence in saying, "I am always very happy." What I can say is that every day is full of moments of happiness, as full as the sky is of stars. Yes, an immense expanse of cold black space yawns out there, but that's not what draws my eye anymore. My gaze, and with it my understanding, have shifted. To believe in God is to believe in good and to see its preponderance everywhere. All I see now are the bright, jewel-like moments of joy that keep coming to me and that, taken together, do not seem a jumble of random sparks but comprise a great and dazzling picture—a vision so beautiful as to utterly overwhelm the darkness.

NOTES

1. Robert Cormier, *Other Bells for Us to Ring* (New York: Delacorte Press, 1990), 116-7.

2. Brian Jones, quoted in Bertrand Piccard, "Around at Last!" *National Geographic*, September 1999, 44.

3. Brother Lawrence of the Resurrection, *The Practice of the Presence of God*, trans. John J. Delaney (New York: Image Books, 1977), 47, 56.

4. *The Book of Common Prayer* (Toronto: Oxford University Press, 1959), 528.

5. Brent Curtis, quoted in John Eldredge, *Wild at Heart* (Nashville: Nelson, 2001), 149.

6. Roald Dahl, *Going Solo* (New York: Farrar, Straus & Giroux, 1986), 112.

7. John Bunyan, *The Pilgrim's Progress* (London: Nelson, n.d.), 41.

8. Found at www.burtrosenberg.com. (A visit to Burt's Web site is a joyful experience in itself.)

9. William Butler Yeats, "Sailing to Byzantium," in *The Collected Poems of William Butler Yeats* (London: Macmillan, 1933), 217.

10. Jerry Spinelli, *Maniac McGee* (Boston: Little, Brown, 1990), 102.

11. E. L. Konigsburg, *From the Mixed-Up Files of Mrs. Basil E. Frankweiler* (New York: Simon & Schuster, 1967), 151.

12. Brother Lawrence, *The Practice of the Presence of God*, 90.

13. M. Scott Peck, *The Road Less Traveled* (New York: Simon & Schuster, 1978), 15.

14. Jim Brandenburg, *Chased by the Light: A 90-Day Journey* (Minnetonka, Minn.: NorthWord Press, 1998), 28, 36.

15. Ron Susek's book *Silent Night, Holy War* has not, as of 2003, been published.

16. T. S. Eliot, *Collected Poems 1909–1962* (London: Faber & Faber, 1963), 110.

17. Franz Kafka, in a letter to Oscar Pollak, January 27, 1904. Quoted in Ernst Pawel, *The Nightmare of Reason: A Life of Franz Kafka* (New York: Farrar, Straus & Giroux, 1984), 328.

18. Robert Brow, *Living Totally Without Guilt* (Kingston, Ontario: Brow Publications, 1983).

19. Keith Jarrett, quoted in Terry Teachout, "Directly from the Heart," *Time,* 15 November 1999, 51.

20. C. S. Lewis, *Surprised by Joy: The Shape of My Early Life* (New York: Harcourt Brace & Co., 1956), 220-1.

21. Norman Grubb, quoted in Dan Stone and Greg Smith, *The Rest of the Gospel* (Dallas: One Press, 2000), 23.

22. To this statement there is one exception that I cover in the Epilogue: The happiest face I've ever seen is that of Jesus.

23. Cynthia Rylant, *All I See* (New York: Orchard Books, 1988).

24. Michael D. O'Brien, *Strangers and Sojourners* (San Francisco: Ignatius Press, 1997), 35.

To learn more about WaterBrook Press and view
our catalog of products, log on to our Web site:
www.waterbrookpress.com

WATERBROOK
PRESS